Sego

by James Sego with Robert Paul Lamb

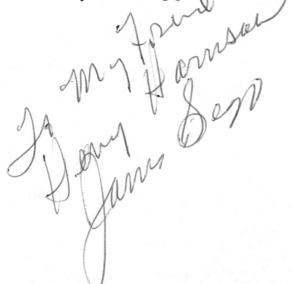

Logos International ● Plainfield, New Jersey

This edition is dedicated to the family, friends and supporters of the Sego Brothers and Naomi, and also to our faithful booking agent, Cecil D. "Sonny" Simmons II.

to Naomi,
who has loved me and cared for me,
in sickness and in health,
for twenty-eight years.

For God so loved the world,
that he gave his only begotten Son,
that whosoever believeth in him should not perish,
but have everlasting life.

John 3:16

Table of Contents

FOREWORD

In the more than thirty years they have been singing gospel music, the Sego Brothers and Naomi have amassed an impressive collection of over fifty record albums to their credit. Their music has a distinctive "clap-your-hands, pat-your-feet" sound that warms the heart and uplifts the soul. It is a much needed sound for the the day in which we live.

No singing group could last for thirty years without having something special. In the Segos' case, I believe it is a calling of God plus the anointing of the Holy Spirit. Those two factors make a dynamite combination in a singing group or a preacher of the gospel.

The Sego Brothers and Naomi have been frequent guests on the "PTL Club" and I have especially enjoyed their appearances. Their old-fashioned brand of gospel singing brings back fond memories for me. It's the kind of music I was raised on.

But aside from the Segos' music, there is another story. It belongs to James Sego, the group's leader, who in his own words was "a stone cold alky" while singing gospel music. Written with my good friend and co-author of my books, Robert Paul Lamb, this book demonstrates the power and grace of God working in a man's life.

James Sego's incredible story of deliverance from the demon forces of alcohol should be great encouragement to every person who has ever wrestled with this problem, or had a loved one who was afflicted with the sickness.

This is a tremendous story that reaffirms the great love God has for His children. I am always inspired when I read just such a story.

JIM BAKKER
host of the "PTL Club"

PREFACE

James Sego's stationery probably says it best—"Sego Brothers and Naomi, Gospel Singers."

I know of very few people who *are* what they want to be in life. Most folks are unhappy with the way their lives have turned out. Many are still searching for themselves. Not James Sego. He is a gospel singer, and that's what he always wanted to be.

The underdogs of the world can take comfort in Sego's story. He has succeeded in gospel music against all odds. In the beginning, the popular groups shunned him. His alcoholic days nearly ruined his health, and two paralyzing strokes almost killed him. Yet, he continued.

His performances are remarkably free of the antics I saw at many gospel sings. He doesn't dress fancy or resort to stage acrobatics like jumping off the platform, microphone in hand, trying to hug and kiss folks in the audience. Nor does he have "shouting fits" as one singer described himself as having. Nor does he engage in saccharin sweet testimonies that lack reality. Sego and his group simply belt out the gospel in a heartwarming "down home" style. I personally find that refreshing.

During the writing of this book, the Sego's huge Silver Eagle bus blew an engine and had to be towed from Wilson, North Carolina to Charlotte. With my help, the group hurriedly rented a station wagon and sped off to sing in several churches in South Carolina.

For the next three days, the six member group was stuck in Charlotte while Trailways was making repairs on their bus. Several singing dates were missed. During those days, stuck in a cramped motel room, expenses rising, I never heard James Sego complain about his mounting problems. He simply got his bus repaired and went back on the road to sing. To me, that speaks of a man who has a calling in life and wants to get on with the job.

I had serious questions, before writing this book, whether gospel singers actually filled a function within the body of Christ. Yet having traveled across the country with the Segos, many of those questions have been resolved. I saw them reaching people who otherwise might never hear or respond to the gospel message. That alone qualifies them.

In spite of the abuses of some, I believe there is a place within the body of Christ for gospel singers. Even if they are balding, portly, raspy-throated baritones, filled with "Piney Woods" wisdom like James Sego.

Robert Paul Lamb
Charlotte, North Carolina

Sego

ONE

"You Is the Most Different Drunk. . . ."

"Get away from me! No! Don't come near me!"

I was shaking from head to toe as I screamed deliriously at my tormentors. The pounding of my heart throbbed inside of my head. My mind feverishly groped for a sense of reality as my reasoning hovered on the brink of insanity.

The scene before me was terrifying. Fierce, ugly bulldogs stared at me from every corner of the room. Their slobbering mouths grinned insidiously. Any moment I expected them to pounce on me and begin ripping me to shreds.

My eyes raced around the room hopelessly searching for anything that gave a suggestion of normalcy. But the bulldogs were everywhere. I was trapped. There was nowhere to run and hide.

"Leave me alone!" I cried in desperation.

My mind was so intoxicated it couldn't rationalize that what I was seeing was only a hallucination. I was having the d.t.'s (delirium tremens) and the worst was yet to come.

Once again I was suffering because of my insatiable thirst for alcohol. A thirst I had not been able to quench in years.

1

"Sego," a voice penetrated my confusion. "Sego, calm down. Sego, control yourself. Sego. . . ."

A gentle hand reached to grasp my arm but I struggled free. Then a viselike grip held me. A nurse quickly administered an injection and I surrendered to the darkness that silently began to envelop me.

The events of the days prior to being admitted to the hospital had contributed to my unstable condition. The rest of the Sego Brothers and Naomi singing group had gone on the road to fulfill a series of engagements, leaving me behind in the care of my sister, Claudell. Alcohol had ravaged my body to the point that I could no longer travel. I greatly needed rest.

Much of the time I spent lying in bed or on the sofa alone in deep soul-searching. Did I say alone? There was one who was always at my side watching wherever I went—my son's bulldog puppy. I couldn't get away from him. No matter how I tried to avoid the dog—wherever I happened to be in the house—I felt his eyes trained on me.

Sure enough, any time I had that feeling, I'd glance around only to find that dog watching me. His head cocked to one side, his pointed ears perched quizzically atop his head. His piercing black eyes annoyingly watched my every move.

The dog increasingly unnerved me, but that was the least of my problems. My body screamed for alcohol. I felt I had to have it to stay alive. But at the same time I knew within myself it was destroying me. I begged Claudell until she allowed me a sip from the bottle she'd hidden away for such emergencies. She and my wife, Naomi, knew there had to be a "spare" around the house whenever my condition worsened.

Finally, one day I realized I had to have professional help.

"I'm going to the hospital," I announced to Claudell. "You can tell Naomi where I'm at when she gets home. I've got to lick this thing once and for all."

"I'll take you there, James," she replied, sounding almost relieved. "Get your things together and I'll call the doctor for you."

This wasn't my first trip to the Peachtree Street Clinic in Atlanta. I had been there several times before "drying out" from a drinking binge. But lately the binges were coming with increasing frequency.

The hospital staff was ready for me. Soon after arriving, the usual routine of tests was taken. A succession of nurses brought countless pills to help me during the time my body would be struggling against withdrawal from alcohol.

A couple of days passed quietly. I felt well enough to venture out into the green-carpeted hallways. But strolling down the clinically white corridors, I suddenly got disoriented. Every corner looked the same. Walking back towards what I thought was my room, I completely lost my sense of direction. Moments later, a nurse found me sitting on a bed in the wrong room.

"Why don't you just go down to the recreation room?" she gently coaxed. "The others are watching TV there."

"That's kinda stupid of me going into another guy's room," I admitted to the nurse as she helped me negotiate the hallway. "I don't usually do things like that."

It was in the recreation room where I first had the delusion of the bulldogs. The television set blared. Guys smoked and talked. But suddenly I noticed these bulldogs looking at me from underneath a couch. I looked around. Nobody else seemed to notice the dogs. But they were plain as day to me.

"There's something wrong here," I said. "There's something bad wrong here."

The others looked at me. Before I knew it, the bulldogs were rushing at me. I kicked and slapped at them, screaming at the top of my lungs.

Two white-coated attendants had me in tow quickly. "There's something wrong here," I mumbled.

"Yeah, we know," they agreed.

A needle jabbed into my arm and darkness fell upon me. Hours later, the sedative began wearing away and I was in for a rude awakening.

I surfaced to consciousness only to find my condition had deteriorated. Propping myself up in bed, I looked and in front of me—worse than before—were the bulldogs. Where there had been only a few, now the bulldogs seemed to have multiplied.

There were dozens of them leering at me from every corner of the room. They were under the couch, the dresser, the night stand. They were everywhere.

Their bulging eyes glared hauntingly at me. Their massive heads loomed out of proportion to the small pointed ears perched on top. Their lower jaws projected forward. Their upper lips curled back as they snarled, showing sharp, uneven teeth. They seemed so real. I could see their sides heaving in and out as they panted for breath and I could almost feel their hot breath on my face.

"If one of those bulldogs bites me, his grip will be hard to break," I reasoned to myself fearfully.

Suddenly the scene became more grotesque and distorted as thousands of snakes wriggled from between the mouths of the sharp-toothed bulldogs. Gooseflesh covered me as the snakes glided across the floor towards me.

I drew up my feet in the bed and shuddered. But they slithered right up onto the bed and in a moment I felt their cold, glassy-slick bodies all over me.

In the midst of the hallucination, a card flashed before my eyes. The kind of cards used in Sunday school to teach Bible lessons. The picture was Jesus knocking at the door. I looked at the Lord's face. He desperately wanted the person to come to the door.

Jesus!

"Yes, that's who I need," it swiftly came to me. "Jesus is who I need."

I turned on the snakes and bulldogs. "In the name of Jesus," I screamed, "get off me. Leave me alone. Get away from me."

"Sego! Sego!" a voice penetrated my illusory realm. It was Thomas, an elderly black man who was a hospital orderly. He had been summoned to my bedside to sit with me.

"Sego, get hold of yourself." His big, brawny hands tried to restrain me as I kicked and swung at the dogs and snakes. Finally, he strapped me to the bed. I could hardly move.

Snakes still seemed to be watching me. "In the name of Jesus, you're not going to get my soul," I cried out. "I belong to the Lord."

I squeezed my eyes tightly shut to keep from looking at the slimy creatures. Demon powers within the animals talked back. "Yes, yes, we'll get you. We'll get you. . . ."

I forced my eyes back open. Once again, I saw the card before me. Only this time, Jesus wasn't knocking on the door. He had his arms outstretched, palms up and open. His eyes were filled with love and compassion. "Jesus!" I cried.

At the mention of His name, instead of crawling, the snakes raced back into the bulldogs' mouths for refuge. If I relaxed from praying, out they came slithering back on my bed.

I cried awhile, then prayed awhile. Time seemed motionless. I was unaware that perhaps twenty or more hours had passed. The last shift of the day changed and Thomas was back again. The shakes were finally leaving my body.

"Sego," Thomas said softly in his south Georgia drawl, "I ain't never seen no man pray so hard in my whole life. You is the most different drunk I ever seen. Yes, you is."

He was right. I was a drunk and I was different.

His words sunk into me. "Here I am," I thought to myself, "tied to a bed with the d.t.'s, a gospel singer in a hospital for drunks. Boy, I've really done it this time."

"Thomas," I agreed, "I am different and I am a drunk."

He nodded. "Yassuh."

"But I ain't supposed to be in a place like this. A hospital for drunks. That ain't no fit place for a man of God. The Lord's called me to carry the gospel in song. I've been on the top, traveling, making records, seeing souls won to Jesus.

"Man, I know the power in the name of Jesus. That's why I was praying so hard. The devil and all of hell are afraid of the name of Jesus. Whether it's snakes, dogs, or pink elephants, they've got to respond to the name of Jesus."

Thomas began to weep. "You gonna be all right, Sego," he said, with tears trickling down his cheeks. "You gonna be all right."

As I lay in bed, I made a promise. "Lord, that's the last one I'll ever do. I'll never get drunk again. I'm stopping right now. They'll be no more for me."

Of course the Lord knows everything—past, present, future. He obviously knew I'd continue drinking. I wouldn't quit easily. He knew I'd return to the hospital time and time again, wasting away to skin and bones because of alcoholism.

How had all this happened to me? I had every reason in the world not to be in a place like this. Mama and daddy had been singers and preachers of the gospel. I had been raised in a Christian home. I'd heard the gospel message from A to Z. My earliest childhood memories centered around church revivals, brush arbors and gospel sings.

My recent success in gospel music gave me even less cause to be in a hospital for drunks. My group, the Sego Brothers and

Naomi, had finally broken into the big time even though we'd been singing together for years. We were known from coast-to-coast through the song, "Sorry, I Never Knew You." We had sold over a million records of that song—the first time any gospel group had reached that mark. Now the words to that song haunted me every time I heard them. They reflected my own spiritual condition.

Everywhere we sang—in churches or concert halls—the places were usually packed to capacity. Our "down home" way of singing was a blessing to young and old alike. We were looked upon as special folks, anointed of God to sing the gospel.

But here I was in a hospital for chronic alcoholics. Sick and beaten down, I had many regrets about yesterday and little hope for tomorrow. Even though I had sung His songs for years, Jesus was not real to me. I thought I'd surrendered my life to Him, but that seemed like a faded memory now.

TWO

Son of a Holy Roller

"I hope it's a boy," Hettie whispered to Claudell and Blondean as they were ushered out of the house to stay with neighbors when mama's birth pains began. The family doctor was on a fishing trip so daddy had sent for "Aunt Bessie," an elderly black midwife.

Mama and daddy were praying for a boy this time. Three daughters and a baby girl stillborn had caused their faith to waver some, but both insisted God was going to give them a boy this time.

Daddy anxiously paced the living room floor of the small frame house the Sego family called home in the farming community of Enigma, Georgia. All the while he was thinking "what a help a boy would be in handling the farm chores." He was a farmer and a part-time Holiness Baptist preacher back then in the year of 1927.

That sunny first day of October seemed even brighter when "Aunt Bessie" finally stepped into the living room drying her hands on a small towel. "Well, Preacher Sego," she announced, beaming, "you've got yourself that boy you been

9

prayin' for." Daddy was fit to be tied when I was placed into his waiting arms.

Mama was Lona Leone Erskine before she met and married James Walter Sego in 1914. Her family had moved from Joplin, Missouri, to Rochelle, Georgia, years before that. The Erskines were sawmill operators and the prospects for a lucrative timber business beckoned them. Georgia was filled with endless acres of pine trees.

Mama always recalled that the Erskines were mechanically inclined people. A distant uncle designed a six-cylinder engine called the "Erskine Six" and sold it to the Studebaker Car Company. But I guess mama was on the "across-the-tracks" side of the Erskine family—we were poor.

After the Erskines moved to Georgia, mama and her sister, Jackie, came to know the Lord. For several years, the two sisters sang gospel songs and preached revivals throughout central and south Georgia. It was at one such revival near Rochelle that mama met daddy. His family was from nearby Vienna where they farmed.

They moved to Rochelle where daddy got a job at a sawmill in 1914, but it was two years before my father became a Christian. Thereafter, he and mama served as itinerant evangelists preaching the gospel whenever a church opened its doors. Aunt Jackie joined them many times until 1926. She was in Miami preaching a revival in September when a hurricane blew through. Mama never heard from her sister after that. The family always presumed that she was among the hundreds killed.

The sawmill business evaporated near Rochelle in the early 1920s, so mama and daddy moved south to Enigma. There daddy farmed and preached, and I was born.

He introduced me to farm life when I was two years old. He would often pick me up with his work-hardened arms, sling me onto his broad shoulders and carry me through the back fields to the pasture. Cows lay in the shade of pine trees and meandered about chewing their cuds. Pigs rolled and wallowed in the mud, growing fat for the slaughter. Those trips through the fields at feeding time grew to become the highlight of my day.

I soon learned to toddle along beside daddy, holding onto his big hand and stumbling occasionally over a big clod of red Georgia clay.

While I was still a toddler, I began to venture away from the house alone. Mrs. Hancock, our closest neighbor, soon grew accustomed to the sight of me waddling—diaper sagging—over to her house each day. The enticement for these trips lay in the teacakes that came fresh from her oven.

I soon was everyone's favorite. My three sisters always seemed to be fighting over me, wanting to take me with them wherever they went. They thought I was about the prettiest thing that had ever been born. Actually I was red-headed, freckle-faced and surely about the ugliest kid you'd ever seen. But as you can gather, my looks didn't hold back my popularity.

We lived in Enigma the first three years of my life until the effects of struggling with a growing family during the great depression proved too much. Finally, daddy gave up farming and the family moved to Empire, about thirty miles south of Macon.

But things weren't any easier in Empire than they had been in Enigma in those waning years of the depression. Jobs were very scarce. Unable to find work, daddy decided to start a grocery store. Since the little community where we lived didn't have one, that sounded like a good business venture.

A small, empty building was acquired and soon shelves were stocked with groceries and daddy's store opened for business. But right from the start the grocery store proved to be a losing proposition.

The problem was that the local people still depended on the town drummer. He drove regularly through the neighborhood in his Model-T truck loaded with fresh fruits, vegetables and staples such as sugar and flour. Over the years, housewives had grown accustomed to the convenience of being able to do their grocery shopping from their front door or out at the curb in front of their homes. Competition was keen.

Daddy found out after a short while that he couldn't exist on the small income from the grocery store and tried to find other ways of supplementing his income. The fact that he had even a modest salary prevented him from getting a job with the Works Progress Administration. The WPA was a government financial program created under President Roosevelt for providing employment to the millions of American citizens still out of work following the depression.

After operating the grocery store for several months in the red, daddy finally had to admit defeat. He sold out his stock, settled up with his creditors, and turned his customers' accounts over to the drummer.

We hadn't had time to make roots in Empire before the next thing I knew we were on the move again. Everything which could possibly be taken with us was loaded on the Model-T Ford daddy had just purchased for forty dollars. This was the first automobile we ever owned and I though it was about the most beautiful car in the world.

As we chugged down the road, we must have looked like traveling gypsies. Bags, boxes and furniture were tied on the fenders, running boards and loaded on top. Small happy faces seemed to appear from every window as we journeyed toward our destination of Adel, sixty miles west of the giant Okefenokee Swamp. Two years before in 1931, Lamar had been born. Now a new baby brother, W.R., rode up front in mama's arms alongside daddy.

Living quarters had been secured by daddy in advance of our move. He had scouted the town and found an empty dance hall. He had seen possibilities which others had overlooked in that vacant building. The place had been empty since the days of the Roaring Twenties when the fads of the dance marathons—the Charleston, the Fox-trot, and the Big Apple—were in bloom. It had crashed like the stock market and everything else in 1929.

"This is the place," daddy exclaimed enthusiastically as the old Model-T rolled to a stop. "Everybody out, we've got a lot to do."

Several moans were heard from the back seat as our eyes scanned the scene before us. The place was an eyesore—the result of vandalism and years of neglect. The broken windows, bashed in front door and generally ramshackled appearance of the dance hall verified daddy's words. There was a lot to do.

The staccato sound of hammers and the rhythmic pull of saws reverberated throughout the rafters of the hollow, empty building. Partitions were set in place which created an auditorium for church services in front and a parsonage for the preacher's family in the rear. A plywood pulpit sat atop a small, raised platform. And the pews were set in twin rows built from knotty pine sheeting. Daddy could now hold church services.

The word that the old dance hall was being converted into a church had already spread throughout town. Very few ventured into the building for the first service, but when God began blessing at the little makeshift church, spiritually hungry souls soon found their way there.

I spent most of my daylight hours down at the swimming hole of a nearby creek. Several of the older boys had built a dam across the creek with flat rocks and some old logs which had washed onto the banks from a flood back in the spring.

Catching crawdads, tadpoles and gigging frogs provided many delightful moments for me. Sometimes after dark I'd sneak out to meet my friends and we'd go back to the creek to hunt for turtles.

Summer soon passed. Fall meant a return to school. When winter came, the wind whipped through the cracks of that old dance hall putting a chill in your bones. That winter happened to be one of the coldest in a long time. Nonetheless, we made it through.

Times became very trying for everyone throughout the depression and for a long time afterwards. Contributions to daddy's fledgling ministry were so meager he tried to supplement his income as best he could. He worked here and there at assorted jobs. An opportunity to work on the local doctor's house was presented and daddy taught himself carpentry.

In time, he became a fairly skilled cabinetmaker. When carpentry work and cabinetmaking slacked off, daddy sought work elsewhere. At times, his search led him fifty or sixty miles south into northern Florida.

Our situation improved enough until we were able to afford a better house out on Highway 41, south of Adel. Perhaps we would have had more if it hadn't been for mama and daddy's generosity. It seemed the house was always filled with strangers.

People were traveling everywhere at the time looking for work. When they arrived in town, they usually went to the police station for a handout and a place to spend the night. After the jail got full, the police chief sent them to the holiness preacher's house. That meant daddy and mama—and they never said "no" to anybody.

I never knew what to expect. I might be in bed one minute and the next minute sleeping on a pallet on the floor. Mama was always adding water to the soup or making the gravy thinner to stretch our meals to provide for unexpected guests.

Financial circumstances forced the sale of the old dance hall building. But that didn't create problems for daddy. He simply began to pray for God to provide another place for his congregation to meet.

"Brother Walt," a man in the church told him, "why don't you take a look at the old blacksmith shop? It's not doing anything but just sitting there. If you want it for a church, I think it'll do just fine."

The idea pleased daddy and off he went to investigate. If the dance hall had been an eyesore, then the blacksmith shop had to be a festering cancer.

Dim rays of sunlight filtered through the filthy windows onto a disheartening scene. Dusty cobwebs drooped loosely between rough, smoke-blackened overhead beams. Dirt and soot lay in windowsills and heaped up in every nook and cranny. The uneven earthen floor lay cluttered with rubbish.

The task of cleaning the blacksmith shop was a monumental undertaking. Daddy, mama and all of the kids who were old enough to use a mop or broom set ourselves to the task. I'll admit my enthusiasm was in no way to be compared with my parents'.

Daddy's newly-developed skills as a carpenter were tested as he attempted to create a similitude of a church from the old blacksmith shop. Benches from the dance hall were set in place facing the well-used plywood pulpit. To the critical eye, however, there was nothing to suggest that this was now a place of worship.

"I know this ain't much," I heard daddy say, "but Jesus promised that where two or three are gathered together in His name, there He would be in the midst."

Daddy obviously concluded that the Lord was true to His

word. Before long it seemed like we were having church all the time. Sunday. Monday. Most every day of the week. People just stayed in the church with no regular hours. There were people there from sunup to sundown praising and blessing God, running and shouting up and down the aisles, weeping and testifying.

A new world opened up for me when I started attending grammar school. I didn't know there was any kind of stigma attached to the name "holy roller" but I soon discovered there was.

I had already had a few problems in school to start with. It was the first day and the teacher had asked my name.

"James Lee Arnett Sego," I replied proudly. That brought a burst of smothered laughter and giggles from the class.

"Why are they laughing at me?" I wondered.

The minute school was dismissed, I ran toward home as fast as my small legs could carry me. Tears streamed down my flushed cheeks. I raced into the kitchen and grabbed mama around the waist.

"Mama, why did you have to name me James Lee Arnett Sego?" I questioned, holding onto her tightly.

Gently she held me away from her and knelt down. Looking me straight in the eyes, she said, "Listen here, James, ain't nothing wrong with your name. It's a fine name and you got nothing to be ashamed of. Now you just quit crying and go back tomorrow and hold your head up high."

I returned to school and that's when problems developed over being a "holy roller." It all started at recess. "Hey, you," a tough-looking kid with a smirk on his face shouted. I looked around to see if there was a possibility he was talking to anybody else but me.

"Yeah, you," he sneered. "I hear you're a holy roller."

I didn't like the implications he made. "No, I ain't. I don't know what a holy roller is but I ain't one of them."

"Yeah, you are," he insisted.

From then on, kids taunted and jeered at me during lunch and recess. One day the problem reached a head. Walking home down a gravel road with the other kids, one of the girls prodded her boyfriend to pick a fight with me.

"Hey, James Lee Arnett Sego," he mocked, "you're a no-good holy roller."

I kept walking, wondering what I was going to do.

"Hey, holy roller, what's the matter? Think you're too good to fight?"

I looked around to see if anybody would offer help. All the kids stood back watching me. I knew I was alone and being tested. I searched frantically for some weapon of defense. Stuck between the pages of my reading book protruded a nice, new, well-sharpened pencil. I pulled the pencil out of my book. When the older boy suddenly jerked me around, I stabbed him solidly in his seat.

Then I ran down the dusty road, my feet flying as if they had sprouted wings. I didn't look back until I reached the house and slowed to a walk. Then I sauntered casually into the house. My intentions were to seek refuge in my room.

But as I walked past daddy who sat in his mohair chair reading a "Grit" newspaper, guilt overcame me. I hesitated. Looking down at the floor, I began drawing imaginary patterns with my foot.

Daddy looked up. "How was school today, Brother?" (Brother was my special family name.)

"Daddy, I done something terrible," I blurted out.

"What'd you do, son?" Daddy lay aside the paper and looked seriously at me.

Tears welled up in my eyes and brimmed ready to overflow. "They kept calling me a holy roller. Daddy, I had to do it."

"What'd you do?"

"I stabbed a boy with my pencil," I revealed as I dropped my head waiting to be sentenced for my crime.

After a long thoughtful pause, daddy reached out and pulled me onto his knee. "Son, the greatest tribute someone could ever pay you is to call you a holy roller."

"Really? Truly?"

I beamed with joy then. I knew what daddy had said changed everything. He was a smart man. I felt he knew everything I needed to know. If being called a holy roller was all right with him, it was all right with me. I grabbed him around the neck.

My joy was short-lived though. He took me by the hand and started out the door. "Where are we going?" I questioned.

"We're going to make sure that boy is okay."

"Do we have to?" I moaned. One look at daddy told me the answer and away we went.

To help out with the pressing financial situation, I started work while in the second grade delivering groceries. I worked every day after school and from 6 A.M. to 9 P.M. on Saturday. The three dollars a week I earned made me feel like a rich man even though I was just beginning to realize how poor my family was.

We had moved again out of town near the city campgrounds. The once glistening, white six-room house had suffered the ravages of changing seasons and over the years had taken on a slate gray appearance. The banisters around the front porch showed gaps from missing slats. Inside the house, mama had to scrub hard to keep clean the well-worn pine subfloor with its many cracks and knots.

One day I arrived home from school to see a strange car parked in front of the picket fence which guarded the yard. Some of our chickens clucked aimlessly about. I walked around the car examining it—feeling the shiny finish beneath the dust which had settled on it from traveling the road that ran past our house. Wiping my hands on my patched jeans, I sauntered into the house.

"Mama, I'm home," I yelled, slamming the screen door behind me. I looked to see a small mustached man sitting and talking with mama. "I'm sure you're gonna be happy with your purchase Miz Sego," he was saying.

I heard no more. I about went into orbit when I spied the new linoleum rugs on the floor. The bright colors and patterns seemed to sparkle in the sun-reflected room.

"Son, this is the linoleum rug salesman, and he's just sold us rugs for every room in the house."

"Sure enough? All over the house?"

I waited to hear no more. I had to see for myself. I flitted like a butterfly into every room in the house. I got down on my hands and knees peering at the patterns from every angle. I knew we had struck it rich. "How on earth could mama afford all this beauty?" I wondered.

I soon found out we weren't rich. At least I couldn't quit my job. I secretly wanted a bicycle but the money just didn't hold out for things like that. Delivering groceries was hard work and I really wanted to quit. Even after working most of the day, I still went to church at night with mama and daddy.

They taught us that being poor didn't matter but being together did. One of the things we did together was singing. After supper each night and after daddy read from the Bible, the whole family gathered around the fireplace and sang. Since we didn't have electric lights, daddy allowed me the honored position of holding the kerosene lamp so mama could read the music as she played away on our old pump organ.

I loved to join in with daddy's deep melodious tones, mama's high tenor and my sisters all blending in with alto harmony. To me, that was the best time of the day.

THREE

Snake Handlers, Brush Arbors and Gospel Sings

Church was the center of our social life as well as our spiritual existence. There wasn't much else to do except go to church in the early 1930s, so it wasn't surprising when Andrew Easters (Naomi's daddy) came to the house one day inviting us to go to a revival meeting.

"Brother Sego, there's some new folks down the road, a clan of people named Hawkins, who just moved into the River Bend area. Wanta go to a meeting they're a-holdin' tonight?"

Daddy was ready to go to church at the drop of a hat—anywhere. In a short time, Mr. Easters, mama, daddy, two of my sisters, plus Lamar, W.R. and myself all piled into the pickup truck along with two guitars and daddy's big bass drum.

River Bend was a community near Brushy Creek, about seven or eight miles from Adel. Jostling along for several miles on dusty back roads, we arrived with little time to spare before the meeting started. The small weather-beaten church with its crude vertical slabs of pine and its galvanized tin roof was set back in a clearing surrounded by a dense grove of tall, slash pine trees.

Cars, trucks and a few mule-drawn wagons were scattered helter-skelter about the church or parked haphazardly alongside the dirt road. It looked like opening day at the county fair.

"I've never seen this many cars and trucks in one place before," I exclaimed to Hettie.

"Maybe they came to hear us sing," she joked, jumping down from the truck.

"Hurry up and get the instruments inside the church," mama prodded.

Daddy and Brother Easters quickly responded with the bass drum. Blondean and Hettie each carried a guitar into the church as mama hustled Lamar and W. R. on ahead. I lingered outside to play as long as possible so when I finally went inside I had to find a seat in the rear. My legs dangling from the split-log benches barely reached the sawdust floor.

The setting sun still provided some light inside as it shone through the two side windows. A set of matching windows on the other side of the building revealed faces of those who couldn't get inside. Coal, oil lamps and lanterns flickered erratically offering their light as soon as the sun set.

The small building was filled with a variety of discordant sounds—people mumbling, babies crying, instruments being tuned. Daddy and Mr. Easters had set up the bass drum on one side of the platform.

A silence swept the audience as a man stepped up to the homemade pine pulpit. "Let us pray now for the Lord to bless our service," he said.

He must have prayed the prayer of faith because I had never seen people get "in the Spirit" so fast. The first song was a lively hand-clapping, foot-stomping number with four-quarter timing. Before the conclusion of the first verse, a few had managed to shout their way into the aisles waving their arms and dancing up and down.

The time finally came for my sisters to sing. They sensed the tempo of the service and began singing "Goodbye, Old World," strumming their guitars in unison. Daddy pounded away on his bass drum, his eyes closed, a smile radiating from his face.

By the time they had reached the second chorus—"I've done left this world behind, I've done crossed the separating line, I've done left this world behind . . ."—a few bolder women began shouting. They seemed to be drawn to the platform, jerking and shaking all the while. Finally they made their way over to a corner where some five-gallon lard cans and burlap sacks were setting unnoticed.

My sisters continued singing—for seeing people shout and dance in response to their singing wasn't unusual. That happened frequently in mama and daddy's services.

A gasp suddenly escaped from the uninitiated in the congregation as the women drew from those cans and sacks some of the biggest rattlesnakes I had ever seen.

Some of the onlookers panicked and began pushing and shoving through the crowd to get out the front door. Others, encouraged by the exhibition, seemed to get "in the Spirit" even more.

I was standing on the bench in the rear completely spellbound. This was the first time I'd ever been to a snake-handling meeting. My eyes must have looked like saucers.

My sisters, who were still singing, had not turned around to see the "demonstration of faith" at the rear of the platform.

One woman danced up near the pulpit with a large rattler laying across her shoulders, its body wrapped a turn around her arm. She held its neck with her hand, its scaly face about two inches away from her nose. Its tongue flicked in and out, its beady eyes glaring.

The singing came to a quick halt. Fear had paralyzed my two sisters' vocal cords! Yet they continued playing mechanically to keep up the rhythm.

As Hettie surveyed those people around her, she saw she was surrounded. Some were holding snakes above their heads. Another had her feet on the back of one. Others simply danced about with their eyes closed, moving rhythmically, snakes dangling about their necks.

"Where's the back door?" Hettie asked, turning to Blondean.

"I looked," Blondean answered. "They ain't got one."

"Well, door or not," Hettie said, trying to stay calm, "I'm getting out of here and fast."

Before I knew what was happening, daddy was off the platform with his bass drum in hand. Mama grabbed Lamar and W.R. and motioned to my sisters and me. Everybody made a beeline for the door.

The balmy night breeze hit our flushed faces as we stepped outside. "Mama, where's Mr. Easters?" I asked, looking around.

"I don't know, Brother," she replied as we hastily walked to the truck. "But don't you worry. He's big enough to take care of himself. He'll probably be along directly."

We didn't have to wait at all. Mr. Easters was already seated in the truck when we got there. He had been in the first exodus of folks when the snakes made their appearance.

The ride home that night produced a few laughs over Hettie and Blondean's paralyzed vocal cords, not to mention Mr. Easter's quick exit.

There was even mention made about one very bold preacher among the snake handlers. He had boasted, "You bring any size snake to church that you can carry. The bigger they are the better I like 'em. If I can't handle 'em, I'll ride 'em."

That was just one of the unusual events that happened as part of mama and daddy's ministry. We met quite a number of rare people in camp meetings, brush arbors and revivals—but that didn't cramp mama and daddy's zeal for serving the Lord. They carried the gospel to several nearby towns every Saturday afternoon in street meetings.

Cecil. Berlin. Norman Park. Omega. Lenox. People in these tiny south Georgia towns always went to town on Saturday. Mama and daddy knew these were ripe moments to present the gospel. Hettie and Blondean opened the programs with song. Daddy preached in one place and mama took a turn at the next. It seemed as if we were in revival meetings all the time. I was taken along without question. During the week, the folks held prayer meetings—and, of course, service on Sunday.

Even though I was in church all the time, I was not always "in" all the time. It was just as easy to let my mean streaks take over as ten-year-old boys will do. I was frequently in trouble with daddy over various scrapes at home or school. One of the incidents came following a double wedding he performed at the house.

As a preacher, people were frequently calling on daddy to marry them. Few weddings were held at church. Most of the folks came to the house. Times were still hard and folks poor so the weddings weren't augmented by rings or flowers. That didn't inhibit daddy's approach. He gave the two couples a thirty-minute wedding sermon. "Marryin' 'em real good," he pronounced.

Seeing everybody was having such a good time I thought I'd add a little something to the festivities. Outside the house, I found a strong log chain in the yard. My uncles used it on their trucks. I tied the chain around the back bumper of a Model-B

Ford, the car the couples were using. I wrapped the end of the chain around a utility pole.

The couples—the Fountains and the McKinneys—smiled and thanked everybody profusely, and started off down the road. The log chain grew taut.

R-R-I-I-P-P!!!!!

The Ford's bumper crumpled and snapped and the car came to a screeching halt. Both couples wound up in the front seat from the jolt. Nobody was hurt, just bruised.

The couples immediately thought some of their friends had pulled the stunt, but daddy—knowing my pranks—didn't look for anybody else. "James, did you do that?" he asked simply, pointing to the bumper now pulled away from the car's body.

I couldn't lie to daddy. "Yes, sir," I mumbled.

When daddy finished with me, I had to eat practically standing up. Needless to say, he married numerous couples after that and I never touched another car.

One summer we moved to Daytona Beach, Florida. A preacher friend of daddy's had convinced him that work was available in the area. Once again, the family loaded up and journeyed South.

Work was as hard to find in Daytona Beach as it had been in Adel so we only stayed six weeks. But during our stay, we were in church services practically every day.

One weekend we had been invited to a camp meeting near Deland where a special Sunday school conference was being held. The big auditorium was packed out as I took my seat with mama and my sisters. Daddy had wandered off somewhere talking with preacher buddies.

As the meeting wore on, I noticed a group of kids gathering on stage and I heard the announcer say something about Daytona Beach.

"Daytona Beach, that's where I live," I thought to myself.

"He must be asking kids from there to come to the stage."

I took off running up to the stage. Mama and my sisters called after me. I pushed past several people on the stage and joined a line of kids stretched across the stage. Each kid seemed to be reciting the line of a poem.

Finally, it was my turn. "Mary had a little lamb," I mumbled, "its fleece was white as snow."

The crowd gasped. People standing in the stage wings were rolling with laughter. I looked back at mama and my sisters. They were sinking down in their seats. My face flushed bright red, the color of my hair. Somehow I had innocently stumbled into a group's performance. I was silently hoping daddy hadn't been looking.

In spite of all my headstrong ways, I knew that Jesus loved me, as He loved all kids. I just didn't realize the full significance of what salvation meant.

But God watched over me. When I was eleven years old, I awoke one day with a high fever and torturous aching in my joints. I had felt twinges of pain a few days earlier but now it felt like fire in my elbows, knuckles, wrist and feet.

Mama and daddy became worried when red spots appeared on my body. My usual lively nature was slowed to a listlessness because of the pain. Finally the family doctor was summoned when my condition failed to improve. After examining me, he made a simple diagnosis—"rheumatic fever."

There wasn't a lot you could do for the disease back in 1938 and I lay bedfast racked with pain for six weeks. Mama and daddy prayed continually for my recovery. Prayer was also offered at church.

One evening a group of folks from daddy's church arrived and gathered around my bed. I lay weak and drawn on a featherbed. As their voices united in a concert of prayer, I, too, begged, "Please, God, heal me."

Then a miracle happened. I instantly became aware that the pain was ebbing from my body. I reached to hug mama who was rejoicing that God had delivered me. An "old-time" camp meeting atmosphere descended on the bedroom filling the hearts of those who had gathered to pray. Their faith had been rewarded.

The pickup pulled in front of the Sparks-Adel High School loaded with the whole Sego family. Daddy maneuvered it into one of the few parking spaces left that Sunday afternoon. I had no idea the day would turn out to be a deciding point in my future.

I had resisted wearing my only suit, a salt-and-pepper shade, but mama had insisted I look nice. "You'll be representing the Sego family and meeting a lot of new people," she had reminded me, "and I don't want anyone thinking you're without proper raising."

Everybody climbed out of the truck. My sisters had their guitars in hand. I carried the picnic basket loaded with mama's hot biscuits and fried chicken. I could hardly wait to sink my teeth into the dinner. The aroma of the warm chicken tantalized my nostrils. This was an annual singing convention and dinner-on-the-grounds and I didn't know how long I'd have to wait.

"Mama, how long will it be before we have dinner?" I questioned.

"Oh, they'll probably have a few songs first, just long enough to give people plenty of time to get here."

I placed the picnic basket on a table under a shade tree and left mama setting the food out. I wandered inside the high school where a crowd was already gathering.

A platform had been constructed in the gymnasium. It was above the floor level, giving the singers a position where they could be seen by the crowd. Microphones and a piano had been set in place.

As I stood watching, a group of men—all dressed alike—assembled at the bottom of the steps leading up to the platform. They waited as an announcer stepped up behind the microphone and introduced them.

"Ladies and gentlemen, we are privileged to have with us today the Smile-A-While Quartet with Deacon Utley."

I had never heard the word "quartet" before but as I watched the men singing I knew it was something special. Unbelievable harmony burst forth from their lips as they sang the famous Stamps-Baxter song, "Give the World a Smile." I didn't believe heaven's melodies could have been any sweeter than those.

It seemed as if my heart melted and poured out of me. I was spellbound and soon found myself praying, "Lord, if you ever heard anybody's prayer, hear mine. Let me be like one of them, 'cause I want to sing like that. Whatever it takes, I'll do it."

Years before when daddy was holding church in the blacksmith shop, a singing group came through on their way from Chattanooga, Tennessee, to Florida. They had sung "Just a Little Talk with Jesus" and as they did, something burned inside of me.

Now that burning came back. I knew then—at twelve years of age—my life's ambition was to sing the gospel. I didn't know how I was going to do it but I knew I would. I was going to become a gospel singer.

FOUR

"Let's Pitch a Drunk"

Shortly after I heard the Smile-A-While Quartet sing in Adel, I began urging Blondean and Lamar to sing with me. Blondean had been singing with mama and daddy since she was six years old and had a good alto voice. With the aid of a Stamp-Baxter Convention Song Book, which we had bought by mail, we began learning the most popular gospel songs.

Singing schools were being conducted all across the South, and Georgia was no exception. These schools, sometimes sponsored by companies like Stamps-Baxter, taught the shaped note method or what we called "harp singing."

If it hadn't been for shaped notes, I'd never have learned to sing properly. The song being learned was first sung through using the names of the notes—do, re, me, fa, so, la, ti, do—as indicated by the shape of the music staff on the song book page.

Sometimes using a pitch pipe, sometimes with Blondean's guitar, we practiced continually. I tried to attend every singing school whenever one was held nearby. And any time a revival, a church sing, or a convention sing was held—the three of us showed up and offered our services.

Soon we didn't have to invite ourselves to churches. They were inviting us. We also began singing on radio station WMGA in Moultrie, some twenty miles west of Adel. The program was our first on radio and was called "Sunday Singing." It was thirty minutes of uninterrupted gospel singing. At first, I was too bashful so Blondean did all the talking for our family group. I was happy just to be singing.

One Sunday afternoon in December, 1941, we were singing "Where Could I Go but to the Lord," when the program was interrupted with a special announcement.

The studio took on a hushed atmosphere as the announcer gave the bulletin. "Ladies and gentlemen, this is a national crisis, the Imperial Forces of the Emperor of Japan have just bombed Pearl Harbor," he said tersely.

Faces quickly turned grim. I had no idea where Pearl Harbor was but that song took on a new meaning to the radio listeners as they faced the sobering reality of being in a World War.

During the next several months, mama went to visit some friends in Macon near the center of the state and came home with news. "Walt, there's a lot of work going on up there, an army camp near Macon and an air base twenty-five miles from town. Why don't we try it?"

Daddy had a limited education and this greatly hindered his job prospects in a small town. Macon was one of the state's largest cities and his chances seemed much better, especially with the military building under way.

"Okay, let's give it a try," he agreed. As soon as he and mama got to Macon, daddy landed a job immediately doing general carpentry work at Camp Wheeler. Things were looking up for the family.

I had been left with Blondean and her husband to help finish harvesting their crops. Mama sent me word to catch a bus to Macon and come to 915 Walnut Street. Wearing my seersucker suit mama had bought on time, I boarded a Greyhound bus for the ride to Macon.

It seemed like I was in a dream when the bus pulled into the blue and white bus station on Broadway. I walked into the bustling station as people scurried by me. Soldiers were everywhere. I couldn't believe it but there was a barber shop and even a lunch counter inside the busy place.

Outside, I peered down the street. It seemed to be filled with tall buildings, some as high as ten stories. I'd never seen anything like this. There were also plenty of businesses catering to the soldiers and sailors—beer joints, military stores, tattoo parlors.

An oversized cop was walking down the sidewalk, nightstick in hand. "Say, boss," I said innocently, "how do I get to 915 Walnut Street?"

He stopped and looked at me and my battered suitcase. "Well, it'll take you a while, if you're walking," he answered. "But if you're riding go down to the corner of Cherry and wait on a city bus. A supervisor down there will tell you which one to board."

"Thanks," I replied and wandered on down the street, all the while looking into the windows of stores. On the corner, I found a man dressed in a blue uniform and carrying a notebook.

"Whatcha looking for?" he asked, noticing my suitcase.

"I've got to find 915 Walnut Street."

"No problem. Just stay right where you are. I'm the bus supervisor. I'll put you on the right bus."

Ten or fifteen minutes passed. Buses pulled to and from the corner, picking up and unloading passengers. Finally, he pointed to a green and white bus as it pulled up. "That's it, just tell the driver where you want to get off."

The driver chuckled to himself when I told him the address where I wanted to get off. "I wonder if he knows something I don't?" I asked myself.

Arriving at 915 Walnut Street, I found the family—mama, daddy and my two brothers—had settled into a large four-story apartment house. The place was so huge and had so many families, it was called "Noah's Ark" by the residents.

"No wonder the bus driver chuckled to himself when I gave him this address," I joked with mama. "He must have been depositing every newcomer in Macon at this spot."

Even with daddy having a regular paying job now, it was still necessary for me to find work and help the family. I was a husky teen-ager and finding work was no problem. Silver's Five and Dime on Third Street hired me as a stock clerk, and later I got a better paying job at Colonial Stores, a grocery chain, working every day after school.

I wanted to play basketball at Lanier High School but my long hours spent working made it impossible. The after-school jobs were like a lead weight on my grades as well, constantly pulling them down.

Even though I tried to keep my nose clean, I was frequently in and out of scrapes in high school. Maybe something about my nature seemed to invite trouble. One of the school's bullies constantly wanted to fight me. But hurting people just wasn't in my nature. Finally I became friends with a hulking football tackle named Bubba. The bully grabbed me one day leaving school with Bubba. In a flash, Bubba hit the guy twice in the stomach knocking the breath and any further trouble from him. Life was a lot less painful with Bubba around.

Perhaps if I had completely surrendered my life to God, I could have avoided a lot of problems. Maybe I could have prevented a lot of heartaches that ultimately came on me when I was older. Even so, I believe God had His hand on me.

Daddy made friends quicker than anybody you'd ever seen. One of them was a Pentecostal preacher we simply called

Brother Hunt. The preacher had a deep love for kids. He and his wife had adopted a bunch of children and his house was a constant beehive of activity. I loved going over there when I wasn't working and constantly begged daddy to let me visit them.

One summer afternoon I was playing baseball near Brother Hunt's house. I slid into third base trying to stretch a double into a triple. A piece of broken milk bottle partially buried in the dirt cut into my knee and took the whole knee cap off. It must have severed a main artery.

Too numb to scream, I watched the blood spurting out. "I'm going to bleed to death in a few minutes," I thought.

"Where's pa?" one of the boys asked.

"I'll get him. He's in the house getting his sermon for tomorrow," was all I heard.

It seemed like an eternity before Brother Hunt ran up to me. "What's the matter, James?" he asked, looking into my pale face.

"Brother Hunt, I think I've cut my leg off," I winced.

Quickly examining my bleeding leg, he knew the situation was desperate. He raised his hand toward heaven. "In the name of Jesus, stop this bleeding," he said strongly.

As he spoke with eyes closed, he placed his hand on my knee. I panicked at his touching the open wound, but to my amazement, I looked and the bleeding had stopped.

"It's true. It's real. Jesus is real. He heals."

For the next few days, I stared almost continually at my knee wondering how Brother Hunt had stopped the bleeding and healed me. I asked him as soon as I could return to his house. "Brother Hunt, what'd you do to heal me the other day?"

"Son, I didn't do nothing. I just acted on faith in the Lord. That's all. You aren't hurting anymore, are you?"

"No, sir," I replied. "There's just a little scar on my knee.

That's the only mark there is."

With miraculous experiences like that plus mama and daddy's faithfulness in their church work, I should have surrendered my life to the Lord. But I was a rebel at heart. Having fun and playing pranks became uppermost in my mind. I knew enough about the Bible to know I wasn't a "saved" person.

Life seemed to fall into a monotonous routine of going to school, to work and to church. Whenever mama or daddy held a special church service somewhere, I usually went along to sing with other members of the family.

Yet when a friend named Sambo suggested "pitching a drunk," I surprisingly listened. Why, I'll never know.

"I don't know about that, Sambo," I replied when he first offered the idea.

"You ever got drunk before?" he quizzed.

"No, I ain't," I admitted. "What's it like?"

"It's fun."

"Well," I agreed, "I'm for anything that has fun in it. Let's go."

"Good," he responded. "You won't forget this. We'll get together after the football game tonight."

That night our team was to play Tech High in Atlanta and I was in the band. I played the French horn. Our team lost the game and the band didn't do much better. "I've had bands for twenty years," the band director said afterwards, "but this has got to be the sorriest one I've ever had."

That wasn't the only thing lost that night. After drinking a fifth of Georgia Boy Corn Whiskey, I was never so sick in my life. I threw up the whiskey along with my supper.

We left the stadium that night and went to a popular teen-age hangout, the "Pig 'N Whistle" restaurant. Sambo produced the bottle with a sly grin. The label had a picture of a man in overalls and straw hat.

"How much do I need?" I asked.

"Just get you a whole glassful," he suggested.

I poured a glassful and looked at it. What did I have to lose? I turned it up and took a long, hard swallow.

Fire raced down my throat sending hot blood through my veins. It was as though someone had set fire to me. I began to light up on the inside. I felt like a new me as I took another long swallow.

After finishing that glass, I drank another one. Before long, I lost realization of where I was. Fortunately, we stayed overnight in Atlanta. My head still throbbed when I reached home on Saturday.

After that first experience with whiskey, I determined to be more careful with how much I drank. I knew that liquid was volatile. It had to be handled with care. But I did like the warm feeling whiskey gave and that led to further experimenting in the weeks that followed.

I'd get with the other boys and sample various brands of whiskey and beer. Four Roses. Pabst. Miller. Champagne Velvet. Naturally, I tried to hide my activities from mama and daddy. I fretted about them ever finding out.

Finally, one night, it seemed there was a plentiful supply of whiskey. The bottle kept being passed to me. I never paid attention to how much I drank but when I stood up, my legs felt like rubber. My vision blurred and flashed off and on like a neon light.

Several guys in the room hooted and howled as I slammed into a door frame. "Hey, what's the matter, James?" one guy laughed. "Somebody would think you were drinking or something."

Someone finally got me to a car and home. At least they must have, the next thing I remember I woke up, sick, in the back of a car pulling up in front of our house.

"You gonna be okay, James? Think you can get in?"

"Yeah," I slurred. "I'll make it."

I staggered up the porch steps and then promptly fell off into the bushes beside the house. My head struck some long forgotten object in the bushes' thickness as I landed.

When I came to, I felt miserable and guilty. "I think I've gone too far this time," I scolded myself. I managed somehow to get into the house undetected. Still dressed, I flung myself onto the bed where I again passed out.

I awoke to the smell of bacon frying and biscuits baking. I barely made it to the bathroom in time before my stomach exploded again in continual vomiting.

Mama heard the commotion and came to the doorway. Tapping lightly on the door, she asked, "James, are you all right?"

Deciding to face the music, I opened the door, feeling queasy and looking like a skid row bum. "Mama, I'm so sick," I mumbled weakly.

She took a long look at my unkempt appearance and scratched face. "Why, Brother, what have you done to yourself?" she asked with a surprised tone in her voice.

"I messed around and got myself drunk," I admitted. "But I ain't gonna do it no more."

"I should say not, Brother," she said with tears glistening in her eyes, "and neither will you run around with that crowd of boys anymore. Do you hear?"

"Yes, mama."

"Son, I want you to be like your daddy. Use him as an example. Don't walk after the example of all these fools."

I closed the door and showered trying to wash away the guilt of what I had done. I felt even worse that mama had found out. She was always grabbing and hugging my neck, and now I had hurt her. She was hurt enough to cry.

At that moment, I decided it would be the last time I'd ever get drunk. "Never again," I promised myself. I had no idea it was only the beginning. The start to a life of misery—all because of alcohol. A life that heaped heartbreak and despair on all those it touched.

FIVE

Naomi

I could hardly wait until I reached my eighteenth birthday. I suppose every boy dreams of the day when he officially becomes a man. At eighteen, my dream was to join the army. I went proudly marching up to the recruiting station on Mulberry Street and with the aid of a beribboned soldier I was a member of Uncle Sam's army in a short time.

After I was inducted, I was first sent to Fort McPherson near Atlanta before being transferred to Camp Pope near Alexandria, Louisiana. I readily adapted to service life and enjoyed being treated like a man. I also continued drinking occasionally—that was part of being a man, too.

However, my dream was soon shattered when Claudell informed me in a letter that mama and daddy were both seriously ill in a Macon hospital.

"James," she wrote, "you're absolutely needed at home. It's a hardship on everyone here since there's no one to provide for the family and expenses are climbing at the hospital. I've contacted mama and daddy's doctor and he's agreed to help you get discharged because of the hardship."

I wanted to help mama and daddy. I guess any child would have felt the same about his parents but it sure was hard for me to give up army life. I'd already made the rank of corporal while still in basic training. But now my army career was over.

After ten months in the army, I was discharged in late 1946 and came back to Macon. I went to work in the signal department of the Central of Georgia railroad. The work—stringing wires and installing power switches along the tracks—was some of the most backbreaking I've ever tackled.

Inside, I still had a burning ambition to sing gospel music and I soon persuaded Lamar and W.R., who were now fifteen and thirteen years old respectively, to join me in a group. Charlie Norris, Jr. was our first bass singer. We called ourselves the Harmony Kings.

We practiced at every opportunity and before long we became part of a radio program called "The Hoedown Party." Two other groups, Peanut Faircloth and his band, plus the Southwind Quartet, also participated.

The program was short-lived, but the Lord had opened our eyes to see the popularity that could be brought with a network radio hookup. We were heard on 458 stations with the Mutual Broadcasting Network. Mail came in to us from coast-to-coast. It thrilled me to see the response as the mail bags came in truck loads almost daily.

Mama and daddy were active at Central Assembly of God in Macon besides doing an occasional revival meeting. But they ultimately grew restless in Macon and decided to move back to Enigma. They were small-town folks and, after all, Macon had 60,000 people. Maybe they were trying to retrace their steps of the past when they were more active in the ministry. I never understood the move, but whatever the reason, the family all joined in to help load the truck and make the move.

Their immediate thought upon getting back to Enigma was

to find a church home. Naturally, we went back to Mt. Zion Holiness Baptist where we had previously attended. The church, along with a string of others throughout south Georgia, had been formed after the turn of the century by Baptists who'd received the message of Pentecost.

The Segos were well known in Enigma since we'd been there on a number of occasions to sing. Andrew Easters, who had been saved under my parents' ministry and had been with us at the snake-handling service years before, still attended the church with his wife, Nona, and six children. We enjoyed renewing old acquaintances with the family. It seemed like we'd known them all our lives.

Of the Easters' family, four were girls—Evelyn, Mildred, Naomi and Margie. Two were boys, Aaron and Gene. One of the girls caught my eye in particular. Fifteen-year-old Naomi had grown into a lovely young woman. She was now an attractive blue-eyed, blonde. My immediate goal was to renew a close acquaintance with her.

I devised a plan of getting my cousin Gladys Cranford to arrange for a date. "I sure would like to date one of the Easters' girls," I told her. "Do you think you could help me out?"

"Which one, James?" she asked, surprised at my interest.

"Naomi. Do you think you could speak to her for me or something and see if she's interested?"

I was thrilled when Naomi accepted. Immediately, I arranged to take her to a school basketball game. From that date forward, I knew there was no one else for me but Naomi. Even though I knew I'd have to wait several years for her to graduate from school, I was willing.

Almost three years passed. The time came for her graduation and we went together to her senior prom. By this time, mama and daddy had moved back to Macon, and I had transportation problems now getting to and from Enigma.

One day I realized I was miserable without her. I nervously picked up the phone, gave the number to the long-distance operator. My heart beat rapidly. My throat went dry as my sweaty hand clutched the phone.

"Hello."

"Naomi?"

"Yes."

"Naomi, this is James. Are you ready to get married?"

All I heard was silence on the other end. I wondered if she had quit breathing or something worse. Maybe she had collapsed from my abrupt manner.

"Naomi! Are you there?"

"Yes, James."

"I mean, after all," I stammered, "we've always talked about marrying and now I don't want to wait any longer."

"Okay," she said, "but you know you'll have to speak to daddy about it."

"Yeah."

I could hardly wait to see her that weekend. I wanted to do the proper thing so I rushed down to Sterchi's Department Store to buy a ring. When I priced them I realized I couldn't afford much. I chose one costing only $67.95, but it looked pretty good. Knowing Naomi, I felt she'd understand my financial situation and wear my symbol of love proudly.

The next plan of action was for me to find us a place to live. I found a modestly priced, furnished apartment on Mulberry Street across from radio station WIBB. Besides working as stock clerk at Colonial Stores, I also did a morning radio program over the station which programed country music primarily.

Gathering my courage, I drove to Naomi's house to speak to her father. She left me alone in the living room with him. I had known Mr. Easters all my life but suddenly I felt like a stranger to him. He soon put me at ease.

"Would it be all right for us," I groped for words. "I mean, Naomi and me want to get married. Is it okay?"

He thought for a minute. "Well, if you want to marry Naomi," he said seriously, "just give me twenty-five dollars and you can take her and Margie both."

I smiled wide. I knew that meant yes.

Brother Davis of the local Church of God officiated as Naomi and I spoke our marriage vows on March 2, 1949, at my sister Hettie's house in Tifton, Georgia. I had ridden a bus to Tifton and arrived for the wedding broke. I had to take a taxi from the bus station to Hettie's. When the driver asked for his fare, I had to borrow fifty cents from several wedding guests to pay him.

Everyone had plenty of advice to give after the service—especially Hettie. "What I need most is money to get back home," I told her, "not advice." Somehow I managed to borrow enough money for one-way tickets for two on a Greyhound bus back to Macon.

Our honeymoon lasted about as long as the cab ride from the bus station to our apartment. The next morning I had to get up for the radio program which was broadcast at six o'clock sharp. I left Naomi still sleeping while I ran across the street to the station. Before dashing out the door, I turned the radio on so she could hear the program. When I arrived back home, we enjoyed our first breakfast as a married couple.

"You're a woman after my own heart, honey," I said when I walked in and saw the breakfast already prepared.

"Aw, James, this is what I want to do," she smiled. "I'm gonna like taking care of you."

My life consisted of being in love with Naomi and singing—in that order. I lived for both. Naomi seemed to understand my consuming desire to sing the gospel. She sat for hours listening to our practice sessions. Her approval of our songs was important to me.

At the time I never dreamed of asking her to sing with us. Never once did I realize she had a good enough singing voice to be working professionally.

In those days of the late forties and early fifties, women generally weren't part of gospel singing groups. There were exceptions naturally. Eva Mae LeFever, Mom Speer and the Carter girls—Rose and Anna of the Chuck Wagon Gang—were the only ones I knew about.

It just seemed as if the all-male quartet was the norm in those days. Thus, it was quite natural for me to ignore a good thing even though I heard Naomi's sweet alto voice constantly singing along with the radio.

SIX

Used Car Dealers, Loan Sharks and Bankruptcy Court

The main hindrance in our life was the fact that at the time of our marriage neither Naomi nor I were Christians. Churchgoers, yes. Christians, no. I knew I should have a salvation experience especially if I was going to sing the gospel. I suppose I didn't think I could live the Christian life and, too, I still wanted to have a drink with the boys every so often.

One night Naomi came home from church to announce, "Well, James, I did it. I walked to the altar and gave my heart to the Lord. I got saved. My heart feels so light and airy. It's the greatest thing that's ever happened to me."

"Well, honey, I'm real glad you did," I answered, looking into her radiant face.

I was sincerely glad for Naomi. I knew her step forward made her a more complete person as I watched her over the next several days. But the gnawing dissatisfaction grew inside of me. Naomi soon became a kind of crutch for me in spiritual matters. I hoped somehow she'd be able to keep me in the good graces of the Lord.

It wasn't long after we married that Naomi felt she needed to get a job to help supplement our meager income. Working at a local dime store served that purpose but the job didn't last long. Quite unexpectedly, Naomi found out she was pregnant.

"Honey, that's wonderful," I shouted when hearing the news. "That's just great."

"Do you really think so, James?" she questioned, looking somewhat apprehensive.

"Oh, yes. I really do."

The following April of 1950 brought the addition of a son to the family. We named him James Carlton. I now had three things I loved—my wife, my son, and gospel singing.

Naomi continued faithful in her church attendance as well as participating in church programs. She also began singing regularly as a soloist or in ladies' trios. At times, she was joined by W.R. and Hettie. Mama and daddy held revival meetings frequently and she went along often to provide special music. Requests grew and they began singing at church homecomings all over Georgia. At the same time, my own group was performing in concerts or various "singing conventions."

I continued running from God, even though I dearly loved to express my soul in gospel singing. If I couldn't do this, I would have dried up like the leaves of autumn. The drive to sing was incredibly strong in my life.

In the back of my mind, a splinter of conscience continually pricked me reminding me I needed God's anointing to be effective in gospel singing. Nevertheless, I ignored its jabs and pushed ahead trying to make arrangements for singing engagements.

Once, when Carlton was nine months old, he came down with what doctors called "influenza meningitis." His temperature registered 106.8 degrees when we finally got him to the hospital. "That temperature is about as high as it can go without the baby suffering permanent brain damage," a somber-faced doctor warned us.

Friends and church folks all over Macon began praying. Daddy made two trips a day to the hospital to pray over the baby. All the while, something told me I needed to "repent and be saved." I wondered if my way of living had anything to do with Carlton's sickness.

Several weeks slipped by. The baby's condition stablilized and he was released from the hospital. Relieved, I quickly forgot about the voice speaking to me about being saved.

We desperately needed transportation for our singing group. I didn't have money to get a good car, but that didn't stop me from trying to keep us in wheels and on the road. I simply headed for the nearest used car lot and made a down payment of fifty dollars with the balance being paid off at ten dollars a week. Off we went down the road.

Sometimes it was great. The people always responded heartily to our singing, but oftentimes their pocketbooks weren't in condition to match their outward enthusiasm. This was the case more often than not.

Finances were only part of the problems. The more recognized singing groups—the professionals who had been at it for years—continually told me what a hard road it was to succeed. With little encouragement from the established groups, I often wondered what I was working towards.

As more money filtered out than came in, there was nothing left for me to do but return the car to the used car lot. With expenses, I couldn't even meet the ten dollars a week payments. Frequently I drove over to the store where Claudell worked and borrowed enough money for gas to wherever we were traveling. Rarely could I ever pay that money back and Claudell never asked. She understood.

Sitting around the house one day being down-in-the-mouth

over the dilemma, I said to Naomi, "Honey, I just gotta do something. I've got to get my group on the road. I gotta sing. I'm going to go get us another car and hope we get enough donations to pay for it this time."

So off I went down the street to the used car dealer again. Third Street in Macon had blocks of them. This time I wasn't as confident as I had been on my first trip there. Obligating myself on the dotted line wasn't the easiest thing to do since I wasn't sure I could back it up. However, the need and desire was there strongly to sing. I felt I had to take the chance.

"Well, boys, here we go," I yelled as I pulled in front of daddy's house. "I've got us a car."

"You think this old thing is gonna hold up," W.R. questioned, looking the car over. "That engine sounds mighty strange."

"Yeah, we can fix it up to run," I assured him. "At least I hope so."

"Yeah, me too," he answered, "but if I was a bettin' man, I wouldn't be taking bets on this hulk."

W.R. had been right. That "fixing" involved an expensive valve job and sent me into the waiting hands of a loan shark. I had to have money to fix the engine and whatever else the car needed. Several hundred dollars later, I ran out of "fixing." I again returned the car, shamefaced this time, as the dealer glared at me when I drove up.

This continued. I'd buy a car, fix it up better than it was when I bought it, find out I couldn't meet the payments, and have to return it.

One day, I drove back to the used car lot. I was once again returning a car. I hopped out and walked toward the well-dressed owner who stood waiting to hear my latest explanation for bringing a car back.

His wide-brimmed straw hat and dark sunglasses offered

protection from the glaring July sun. His face was tanned and lined from hours standing in the sun talking to customers. "Well, Sego," he said, matter-of-factly, "I see you're returning another car."

"Yes, sir, I am," I answered, growing slightly nervous.

"Tell me something," he said, chomping on the stump of an unlit cigar, "how many times have you bought cars from me?"

"Oh, I don't know, maybe four or five times."

"But why is it you keep bringing 'em back?" he asked, scratching the back of his neck.

"Well, sir," I said, trying to read his feelings behind the dark glasses. I hesitated, then decided to tell him the truth. "I'm hauling a gospel quartet in it."

He was silent for a moment, studying the asphalt street where heat waves rolled upward. He took the cigar out of his mouth and spat on the ground. "What's a gospel quartet?"

"Well, it's people that sing songs about Jesus," I said, wondering how somebody could live in the South and not know that.

"You mean sorta like Smile-A-While Quartet?"

"Yeah. Like that." I found myself grinning.

"Well," he asked, slightly puzzled, "don't the people pay you anything?"

I shrugged my shoulders. "Sometimes they do. Sometimes they don't. I just go and sing."

He seemed confused. "But, what do you get out of it?" he probed.

"I don't know. I just like to sing."

He paused again. "Well, why do you keep buying cars when you can't afford 'em?"

I was embarrassed. That was a question I never stopped to consider. "Well, I don't know. I reckon I just want to get my group to where they're supposed to be singing."

He looked at me square in the face, shaking his finger. "You know I've never turned you into the credit bureau."

I nodded affirmation. "Yeah, I appreciate that."

He chuckled. "You know I've sold those cars you've bought and brought back for more than what you paid for 'em. You return 'em in better condition than you bought 'em."

"Well, I try to take good care of the cars."

"I want you to do me a favor," he said, glancing over at the shiny cars on the lot. "Don't buy any more cars from me. You're about to drive my bookkeeper crazy."

"Huh?"

"My bookkeeper—she's threatened to quit. You keep coming in here buying cars and returning 'em. She can't keep up with the paper work." Then he started laughing. "Come to think of it, that woman was nuts before you started buying cars," he admitted.

I was at a loss for words.

"Now, listen," he continued. "I want to do you a favor. When do you sing? Weekends?"

"Yes, sir. Usually I leave on Friday and come back Sunday night or early Monday." I wondered what he had in mind.

"Now will you bring my car back no later than Monday?"

"What car?" I gulped.

"The one I'm gonna let you have right now," he answered, his mouth spreading into a wide grin.

"Oh, yeah," I said, thinking my ears must be deceiving me.

Taking me by the arm, he turned my attention to a row of new cars. Buicks. Cadillacs. Oldsmobiles. Pontiacs. "Look over there," he said, pointing a manicured finger at the cars. "I want you to pick out the one you want and drive it out of here."

My heart skipped a beat and my mouth grew dry. I licked my lips as I tried several times to frame the words that seemed to be stuck in my throat. "Wha-aaa-t? You're kidding me. Aren't you?"

"No, I'm not," he said. "I'll even take out an insurance policy on you while you're using the car. If you want to tell people where you got the car, fine. If not, that's okay, too. I'd just like to be able to help get you where you're going."

"You're really not kidding me."

"No, I'm not," he smiled.

I nodded.

"Only do me a favor," he said, with a touch of pain in his voice, "please don't buy no more cars from me."

"Okay, I won't."

"Now go ahead and get one of those cars."

"Yes, sir, yes, sir," I responded. I walked rapidly across the car lot and then up and down between the cars, peering into the interior of each one. Finally I fixed my eyes on a brand new Cadillac and slid into the driver's seat.

My hands gripped the big plastic steering wheel with its shiny horn ring. The instrument panel looked like the cockpit of an airplane. I moved my hand across the blue leather trimmed interior, and took a swift, appraising look across the plush back seats.

Turning on the ignition, I grinned smugly as the engine purred like a contented cat. I felt like driving on air as I pulled over to the exit. The car dealer waved me on, his smile accentuated by the cigar gripped between his teeth.

"Man, what a way to be traveling to our sings now," I said to myself as the Cadillac breezed along home. Yet, I knew God had His hand in the situation. The car dealer had made a decision totally beyond himself.

I had my car problems temporarily solved but there were still other financial woes to face. Some had become almost irreparable. I was deeply in debt to several loan sharks. And the situation had reached the point that I was borrowing from one to pay off another. If I borrowed $150, I'd end up owing $258 by the time interest was added.

One time I was overdue on a payment to a loan shark. I didn't have any idea where I'd come up with the money. I was getting into my car on Cherry Street when along came the creditor. I knew he was looking for me and I just couldn't face him that day.

"Hey, Sego," he yelled, running up to where I was standing. "Wait a minute. I want to talk with you."

I knew I shouldn't run. It wasn't right but I felt like a treed 'coon with nowhere to run or hide.

"Hey, man, you owe me some money and I want it now," he said firmly.

"But I don't have it right now," I answered lamely. "I'll be in right away and give you something on it."

He stepped closer and grabbed me with a strong, bone-crushing grip. "I said I want the money now," he demanded, shoving his face right in front of mine.

I tried to back away. "Now wait a minute," I pleaded. "Don't get excited. You'll get your money."

His boisterous behavior attracted the attention of passers-by and soon a crowd was gathering. I felt my face burning bright red from all the embarrassment. My eyes searched the crowd looking for help. Suddenly I spotted a policeman making his way through the people. I reacted quickly.

"Hey, officer," I yelled. "Help me."

Startled, the loan shark turned me loose.

"Hold it," the burly policeman demanded as he strode up. "What's going on here?"

"Look, officer," I explained, "I owe this man some money and he's been trying to collect it. The problem is I don't have the money. He's bothering me and I think there's a law or something about trying to collect money from a man on the street."

"Yeah, I think so, too," he agreed. "Come on, buddy, leave this guy alone. You can talk to him later under more favorable conditions—but not on the street."

"Thanks, officer," I offered. Quickly I slid behind the wheel, started the engine and rode off.

Leaving the scene with the loan shark still arguing with the cop, I realized I had to do something about my finances. I had borrowed from one loan shark to pay off another until I had mortgaged every stick of furniture in the house. Yet, I had done it all just to keep the singing group on the road. We had even bought matching suits with some of the money.

A few days later, a loan shark came to the house and menaced Naomi over our mounting debts. She was in tears when I got home. "Singing group or not," I decided inwardly, "it was now time to do something about the debts."

"James, what you need to do is wipe all your debts clean," Virgil Shepard, a lawyer friend told me. "There's a Chapter Thirteen of the Bankruptcy Law and this will give you a fresh start. In fact, I won't even charge you anything to help you out."

"Well, I don't know," I said, pondering the mounting debts. "I don't know what to do . . . maybe I should."

"Okay, we'll notify all your creditors and have them appear in court. I'll set it up."

Virgil arranged everything and my day in court arrived. As I sat waiting for my case to be called, I began looking around. There sat people from every stratum of society. Some, I suppose, with greater needs than mine. I scooted around in the mahogany chair polishing it to an even slicker shine with my coat.

The monotonous voice of a witness now on the stand droned

on. A sleepiness fell on the onlookers. I noticed some of the men to whom I owed money. Some stared sullenly at me. None seemed enthused at being there.

Guilt seemed to wash over me. "Lord, these are people just like me trying to make an honest living," I thought to myself. "I'm not a very good example of a gospel singer—I know that. But I feel as if I'm trying to cheat them."

Somehow I couldn't go through the sham of declaring bankruptcy. I turned to Virgil sitting beside me. He was rustling through his legal papers checking last minute details. Our case was next. I nudged him with my elbow.

"Hey, man, I can't go through with this," I volunteered. "These are human beings like you and me. I don't want to beat them out of their money. I want to drop the whole thing."

"But, James, that's crazy," he said, mystified at my actions. "You're not doing anything wrong. This is perfectly legal. Anyway they'll be calling our case next."

"I know that," I agreed, "but I want to try and pay these people somehow." Glancing around the room again, I felt as if my creditors' eyes were boring holes in me.

"James Sego," the court clerk suddenly announced.

"What are you going to do?" Virgil asked, sounding annoyed.

"Let's forget it," I said.

"Okay, if that's what you want," Virgil sighed, stuffing his papers into a slim briefcase and zipping it closed. He walked over to the clerk handing him some papers.

My creditors looked puzzled as I stood up and walked out of the courtroom. Reaching the house later, I realized there was still no way for me to pay these people. What I needed most was time. With time, I could pay off these debts.

The rest of the day I spent repeating my story seven or eight times to a bunch of startled creditors. "Look, if you'll be patient with me and let me pay just so much a week, I'll pay you off. I don't want to file bankruptcy. I'll do the best I can."

To my amazement, every one of them agreed. They were so shocked at my actions maybe they couldn't figure anything else to do. I had filed for bankruptcy, then walked out of court without even having my case heard. Now I was calling them to agree to pay off the debts.

Fortunately, once the air had cleared, I had their respect and some left over for myself. From that time on, I promised myself to stay away from loan sharks and bankruptcy court forever.

SEVEN

Uncle Ned, the Chief Honcho

My feet carried me swiftly across the street from the radio station and up the steps into the house. "Hey, Naomi," I called as I burst through the front door, "guess what?"

She stepped from our small kitchen into the living room. "What are you so excited about, James?" she asked, brushing a sprig of blonde hair from her face.

"You know WMAZ is putting up a television station out on the Cochran Short Route?" I asked, placing my hands on her small shoulders and looking into her bright eyes.

"Yes, what about it?" She appeared confused at my burst of excitement.

"Well, they're going to have a program featuring Uncle Ned, moving him from radio to television. I guess they must have recognized his popularity. But I think they're going to have a gospel group on the program. I've already met Ned when he worked at the fire department and I see him practically every day at the radio station."

"Do you think you might be able to get on?"

"Well, Ned kinda likes us and our style. I figure we'll have as good a chance as anybody else to get on."

"That's wonderful, honey. I hope so."

I was a little disappointed that her enthusiasm didn't compare with mine. She continued, a wry smile on her beaming face. "Now it's your turn to guess what? I've got a surprise for you."

She stood there looking serene as a madonna. I held her close. I had a funny feeling I already knew the answer but I asked anyway. "What is it, honey?"

We're going to have another baby," she revealed.

My premonition was right but I let her think I was surprised. "That's just great, honey," I said, planting a big kiss on her soft lips.

We sat on our worn sofa holding hands like a couple of high school sweethearts talking at length about our coming addition. Now I could really use some extra money to support our growing family.

"James, why don't you call Uncle Ned up now and see what he says about the group being on the program," she suggested.

"Okay," I agreed, thinking now was as good at time as any to call. I twisted the cord nervously as I heard the phone ringing at the other end. "This could mean a lot to us," I thought, "plus I could use some extra money now with. . . ."

"Hello," came the familiar voice over the line.

"Hello. Ned? This is James Sego. You know me from down at the radio station and the sings at the auditorium."

"Yeah, James, I trust you're doing fine. What can I do for you?"

"Well, I heard about your new television program at WMAZ, Ned. I was wondering if you could use a local gospel group. You've heard us and we'd sure like to get a chance to try it."

"Yeah, I think I might be able to use you, James. Why don't you take a run out to my house and we'll talk about it."

"Sure, I'll be there in a half-hour. Bye."

I hung up the phone almost dazed. "Did you hear, Naomi? Did you hear?"

Appearing on Ned's program was a big boost to us. The program called "Uncle Ned and his Hayloft Jamboree" held an amazing popularity with people all across middle Georgia. Most of the show's interest and popularity centered around Uncle Ned's personality. People loved Uncle Ned.

His real name was Gene Stripling but very few folks ever called him that. A self-taught piano player, Ned cut a rakish figure with his pencil-thin mustache, slicked-down black hair and western outfit. Ned wasn't a singer but that didn't stop him from entertaining the "folks," as he called them, with a song—his hands flying over the keyboard, his foot patting wildly.

Along with that musical touch, Ned had a sense for selling, the likes of which I've never seen. Because of his "down home" personality, he was the kind of guy who could have logically sold deep freezers to Eskimos if he had lived in Alaska. Since he didn't, he specialized in other things—sewing machines, soft drinks, corn meal, appliances, flour. Whatever he was selling, Ned made you want to run out and buy it.

His speciality was Thomas Whole Hog Sausage. Ned would fry those sausages on camera, all the while making your mouth water as he did. "Now treat your old man right, mama," he'd suggest grinning, "and get some of these sausages **t-oo-day.**" I could see the women running to the grocery stores following that commercial.

Our group was just country enough to fit into what Ned was doing. We were invited back week after week on the program, probably more than any of the seventeen gospel groups in Macon at the time. Thinking we were taking up too much time from the program, I approached Ned.

"Ned, I appreciate all the exposure you're giving our gospel group on the show, but I feel like we're cutting some of the country singers and musicians out of their time."

Ned placed his hand on my shoulder reassuringly. "Now you listen here," he scolded gently, "I run this show and I put on what I like. Man, you boys have a good sound and I want gospel music on my program."

Our numerous appearances on the show provided many occasions for contact with professional gospel singers. Since Ned was such a popular entertainer throughout middle Georgia and did frequent in-person shows himself, he was often the first person contacted when gospel singers came to town. Among entertainers, Ned was known as the chief honcho around Macon. With his extensive television coverage and great popularity, he could make or break a show at any of the local auditoriums.

I always felt ill at ease whenever the big name quartets sang on the program. They always seemed aloof and never offered encouragement. To them, we were just another of many local singing groups they saw in every town. I guess we were like the others—just struggling along with hopes of someday making it full time.

Ned obviously recognized my attitude. "Hey, these professional groups are no more important than you boys," he told me one day. "They may think they're something special because they travel around and sing, but back home they're just a local group like you are in Macon."

"Hmmmm," I thought.

"Now I'm not suggesting you act uppity or anything," he continued. "You don't have to humble yourself down to anybody except Almighty God. Just raise your head up, walk out there and sing your best. That's all you gotta do."

Ned seemed to have a unique way of boosting your

confidence. Many times he encouraged us when he had a visiting gospel group on the program. After the group had sung, the camera panned to Ned's ever smiling face. "That's a beautiful song, boys," he'd say, "and I'm mighty proud to have you on the program today. But now friends, here are some people we think are pretty fine singers themselves—Macon's own Sego Brothers."

The usual practice among promoters was to use local talent to warm up the audiences for the professionals. Bringing us on to follow the more established road groups was a shot in the arm to our sagging morale. Having such talent savvy, I'm sure Ned knew exactly what he was doing.

In the years to come I would meet countless promoters and would-be show personalities but none with the warmth, charm and kindness of Gene Stripling. He taught me to believe in myself. And somehow instilled confidence in a group of struggling gospel singers.

The response from the television audience to our singing was overwhelming. The avalanche of cards and letters we received in the mail verified Ned's confidence in us. It also helped improve our singing style and gave us access to better engagements.

Shortly, a highly successful promoter from Tallahassee contracted us to appear on his programs. Even though under the terms of the agreement, we were only the warm-up group for his concerts, the many appearances gave us exposure before increasingly larger audiences in many cities across the South.

Just when it seemed the group was within reach of achieving full-time professional status, discouragements and problems came from all sides. We'd always had changes in personnel. Charlie Norris, Jr. had sung bass and his mother played piano in our first group. Three years later, J.C. Newman began singing bass with Carolyn Schell playing piano. Three more years followed, this time London Parris was on bass and Charles Felty on piano.

But now I faced even tougher changes. Unable to meet his financial obligations anymore, Lamar felt he should seek a more stable income for his growing family. W.R., who had many times voiced a desire to preach the gospel, decided to heed the call to do just that.

But for me, the compelling force to sing the gospel never abated. It was always with me. Clifford Thompson, who had sung with the Smile-A-While Quartet before it disbanded upon the death of Deacon Utley, was forming a new group called the Travelers Quartet. I joined them in 1955 and sang with the group for about two years.

Something was missing though. I didn't feel the same satisfaction I had singing with my brothers. I often wondered if the Sego Brothers would ever re-form. Or was this the end of our gospel singing as a family? Maybe it was even the end of my gospel singing. I had no answers to the questions.

EIGHT

"Here's the Sego Brothers and uh . . . Naomi"

I stared in astonishment at the royalty check I had just received in the mail. The figure on the enclosed check amazed me. I never thought it was possible.

"Naomi, come here and look," I yelled, still staring in unbelief.

"What is it, James?" she asked, walking into the room.

"Look at this," I declared jubilantly. "You ain't gonna believe it." I thrust the papers and check in front of her. "That album is selling like hot cakes."

She quickly scanned the papers and looked up, her excitement mixed with bewilderment. "It's hard to believe, isn't it?"

"Naomi, do you realize what has happened? I don't believe any song in gospel music history has ever sold like this one," I laughed excitedly.

I plopped into a nearby easy chair. "What a break," I exclaimed, "that God gave the Segos and Naomi the privilege of being the ones to record 'Sorry I Never Knew You.' "

Naomi nodded in agreement as we both realized it was this

song that had catapulted us into a new realm of success we were suddenly enjoying.

I lay my head back against the high back of the chair, closed my eyes and let my mind drift back to how it had all begun. It seemed at that moment I could hear mama's voice so plain— "James, you need to let that girl sing with you boys. It would be the best thing that could happen. She's good and you know it." Mama was once again hammering at me.

"But mama, I've two young'uns now. I don't want Naomi leaving our kids at home and spend her time traveling around with us," I had argued.

"But she has such a beautiful voice and since Hettie died she seems to have just given up singing. Why don't you give her a try?"

I protested gently to mama that there just wasn't a demand for mixed groups in the professional field of gospel music. "With just four exceptions," I tried to explain, "Eva Mae with the LeFevers, Mom Speer with the Speer Family, plus Anna and Rose Carter with the Chuck Wagon Gang, there just ain't any women in gospel music."

However, mama's words laid heavy on my heart. It was true Naomi seemed despondent lately. Since the life of my sister Hettie had been cut short by cancer, it seemed something inside of Naomi had died too.

The feeling nagged at her that she could no longer participate in the musical part of a service without Hettie to sing with her. I also noticed that I didn't hear her singing around the house much anymore. This puzzled me because she loved to sing as much as I did.

Naomi did have a beautiful singing voice but I couldn't see any way of using her with the group. The Sego Brothers were back together again after two years of going our separate ways. The addition of Dempsey Rainwater's smooth bass gave

promise of bigger and better things to come for the group.

One evening, while practicing, I wanted to cheer Naomi up so I asked her to sing lead and let the group sing backup.

"You know, James, I like that song," Dempsey's booming voice interjected as we finished the number. "We ought to let Naomi sing that as a special the next time we're on Uncle Ned's show."

"Aw, there ain't nothing special about that song," I protested. "It's just an old song. Why Naomi's been singing it for years now."

Comments by the other members of the group were tossed back and forth. It seemed everybody was in favor of Naomi singing the song but me, so I gave in. Viewer response following Naomi's appearance was tremendous—only it was her first and last time to be on a program with Uncle Ned.

Ned had fallen victim to several minor heart attacks but when the last one came he was dead on arrival at the hospital. The show was canceled.

Ned's death and the show's cancellation affected me strangely. For some reason, unknown even to myself, I sought consolation for my depressed spirit in a bottle. I had turned to drinking more and more lately as the answer when anything upset me.

Whenever I came home drunk, Naomi would plead with me to leave the bottle alone. I knew she was right and for awhile I was able to stay sober.

A bright note of encouragement lifted me from the doldrums when I received a call from Ronnie Thompson asking the group to appear on his new gospel singing program sponsored by Friedman's Jewelers.

Following that Sunday's first appearance, Ronnie met us backstage with a warm smile and a firm handshake. "You guys are great," he said.

"We know it," Dempsey Rainwater retorted as he grinned proudly from ear to ear.

Everybody laughed. Ronnie smiled. "I want you guys on every Sunday you're in town," he suggested.

"We'll be glad to," I assured him.

Weeks later, we were back for another spot on the program. "Hey, Ronnie," I announced when we arrived at the studio, "we're going to let Naomi join us today for a song. She's got one we back her up on and it's pretty good."

"Okay, James, I'll trust your judgment," he replied.

Somehow there seemed something special about the occasion. We stood behind the curtains waiting for our turn to take positions before the cameras. Hearing the first group finish their song, Ronnie moved out toward the camera with a glance backwards. "Get ready," he said.

I straightened my tie, glanced reasurringly at Naomi and listened anxiously for our cue.

Ronnie did a brief commerical, then announced us. "And now, folks, here's Macon's very own, the Sego Brothers and uh . . . Naomi."

I was mildly shocked. I hadn't expected to be introduced that way. My face must have appeared startled when the camera's eyes suddenly glowed red and I knew we were "on the air." Instinctively, the group began singing—blending its harmony with Naomi's voice. Her trumpet-like tones were angelic. I knew from the expression of those in the studio we were good. I glanced to the side and caught Ronnie smiling and flashing an "okay" sign.

As soon as we finished the song, Ronnie closed the program. He came over later and grabbed my hand. "James, that's the most commercial sound I've ever heard."

"Thanks, err-rr, what does commercial mean?" I asked ignorantly. "Is that good or bad?"

"Oh, that's good," he assured me. "Man, you need to let Naomi sing with you guys all the time."

Ronnie's words stunned me. Once again I was being told to let Naomi join the Sego Brothers singing group. "Is somebody trying to tell me something?" I wondered.

"Maybe I'm not really listening to Naomi's voice?" I mused.

But the opportunity came to listen to the group's sound with Naomi when we appeared on some programs sponsored by Lowery Homes. I was able to purchase the tapes of the shows and heard them for myself.

That night, after placing the tape on the player, I stretched out comfortably on the old sofa and closed my eyes. The sounds I heard over the tape player startled me. I sat bolt upright. "Hey, we are good," I said aloud, "especially Naomi."

For the first time I realized Naomi had just the right quality to her voice that would make people want to listen. A quality that inspired and encouraged people while, at the same time, urging them to follow Jesus.

Hours later, after retiring, I tossed and turned in bed. Even though I had no relationship with God, I found myself praying to Him.

"Lord, if it be your will, show me what to do. You know the prayer I made to you when I was twelve years old. I wanted to sing gospel music even then. And now as things are turning out, I see it's possible. I know I'm not living like I should, Lord, but I'm depending on you to help me. I really need some answers."

As the night slipped away, giving place to a new day, I knew Naomi was supposed to become part of the group. We would become The Sego Brothers and Naomi.

It wasn't hard to convince Naomi. She loved to sing and I think she was hoping for this opportunity. Her natural shyness soon melted away when she stepped before a crowd and did what she enjoyed best—singing.

One afternoon at practice we began discussing the possibility of making a record. Dempsey had a suggestion. "Listen, James, if we go ahead, let's do that song Naomi first started singing with us."

"You mean, 'Sorry, I Never Knew You'?" I asked. "Man, I can't see where that song would sell any records. It's too old. Why, Naomi's been singing it in church for years."

Naomi had first heard the song five years earlier in 1954 when a singer from North Carolina, Shirley Black, sang it at our church in Macon. Written by a Baptist preacher, Sherman Branch, the tune was first called "The Dream Song." I couldn't imagine anybody wanting to hear it on a record.

Dempsey was persistent though. "Yeah, but the thing you gotta remember," he reminded me, "is the reaction that song gets when Naomi sings it. You might not be impressed with it but there are a lot of other folks who are."

Using the sound facilities at WMAZ-TV, we recorded "Sorry, I Never Knew You" and three other songs on a 45 rpm extended play record. We sold the records at our concerts and sent them to radio stations that played gospel music.

In the meantime, I began searching for a record company to handle the group. I discussed the situation with Herschel Smith, a friend who handled gospel concerts and was familiar with people in the recording business. In turn, Herschel directed me to a recording executive who he felt would be interested in the group.

I wasted no time in contacting the executive. The first question he asked was, "How good can you guys sing?"

"Very well."

"Yeah, well, I'll take Herschel's word. He says you're what we want and that's good enough for me."

Since we knew little about the techniques needed to

produce a quality sound, we were fortunate to be teamed up with Billy Sherrill, one of the finest "a & r men" and engineers in Nashville. Billy was a genius in producing the sounds we needed.

The album—"Is My Lord Satisfied with Me?"—introduced Naomi and her unique vocal styling to gospel music. As soon as the recording session was over, I could hardly wait for delivery of the album on the Songs of Faith label. During the nine months it took from production to delivery, I awaited its birth with anticipation as eagerly as if it was a new child.

When the album finally hit the market, sales soared immediately. Every song on the record was turned into a single. The album itself sold over 300,000 copies. Everywhere we went people wanted to hear songs from the album.

In the meantime, radio stations in Alabama had begun actively playing "Sorry, I Never Knew You" from our little homemade 45 rpm record. "Have you ever heard of a song called 'Sorry, I Never Knew You,'?" our record producer asked me one day.

"Sure, we've got it on a small extended play record," I said.

"Well, I'm getting calls for the record. I think we ought to do a second album with that tune on it."

Plans were begun immediately to make another album using "Sorry, I Never Knew You" as the title song. Little did we know that this song would account for sales of one million records—the most ever by a single gospel tune.

With the release of the second album, calls began coming from all directions for the group to appear. In spite of the spiritual void in my own heart, it seemed as if God had His hand upon us in a mighty way.

One of the first calls I received came from Herschel Smith who had helped us land a record contract. Herschel wanted us for an upcoming concert in Atlanta to replace a group unable to make the date.

"Do I want to work Atlanta?" I quickly responded across the jangling telephone line. "Do I? Man, that's the gospel singing capital of the world."

I hung up elated. "Thank you, Lord. I sure want to thank you for giving us a chance to sing in Atlanta."

The other members of the group were equally thrilled with this new opportunity. "We are finally making it into the big time," I thought ecstatically.

Standing backstage that night in Atlanta, most of the other groups did nothing to make us think we had made the big time. On the contrary, it seemed as if we were being snubbed. Maybe they considered us amateurs in our mismatched suits. Although we were reaching new heights with our record sales, we obviously lacked a polished look in person. Most of the groups wore look-a-like suits which we couldn't yet afford. Maybe they thought we were trying to be different or possibly they were threatened by our record sales when we weren't even full time yet. The result was mostly the same: people acted as if we had leprosy.

At the end of our first song, the audience's reaction contrasted sharply with the indifference of the other singers. The crowd gave us a standing ovation. It seemed that night as if heaven had sent its sweetest choir director down to anoint us. Our voices blended together in a harmony that lifted hearts heavenward.

As we sang, I caught glimpses of the other groups standing in the wings. They seemed intent on watching us as well as the audience's reaction to our singing.

Listening to the applause, I realized something greater was happening than a crowd clapping for a song. I was seeing a dream come true. "Thank you, Jesus. Thank you, Jesus. You have fulfilled the desires of my heart," was the message I was receiving.

Grinning, I stepped to the microphone and with the spotlight glaring down on me began talking to the now hushed audience. Sweat popped out on my brow. Tears brimmed in my eyes.

"Thank you, ladies and gentlemen," I said emotionally. "I'm glad you like us. We're really feeling this touch of the Lord up here tonight. You know I don't believe in fakery on the stage. If I feel it, I've got to show it. This isn't any time to whine or mope around. This is how we should all feel. . . ."

And we moved into our next song,

"He saved my soul,

"Oh, praise His name,

"I'll never forget the day He came . . ."

That night in Atlanta was the beginning of something special. Suddenly we were being invited to many of the larger gospel sings. We still went to the small churches as well, but for the first time, we were on stage with the more recognized groups.

I might have been singing songs that said "He saved my soul" but I couldn't back it up in reality. That thought constantly nagged me. It was becoming more joyful to sing since we were enjoying a little success but *I* still wasn't right.

Mama and daddy had pioneered a Holiness Baptist church at Third and Wood Streets in Macon. A revival was in progress with a local boy, Larry Ball, leading the services. Larry was just starting into the ministry and this was his first revival. I was getting ready for work one morning when Larry came by the house.

He and I were sipping coffee at the breakfast table. "You know it would be kinda sad to hear all this preaching, have all these preachers in your family, be singing the gospel and still die and go to hell, wouldn't it?"

Larry's question startled me. A few steps away, Naomi was

doing the dishes and I heard her catch her breath.

Most of the family knew I wasn't saved. I tried to hide the fact from others by spending time each night at the altar. Above all Naomi knew the truth better than anybody. She had sobered me up enough to know the sin in my life. I knew she must have been shocked that Larry had the nerve to ask such a question. Nobody had ever done that before. Now the truth was out in the light. I knew she was hoping that I would respond to his pleading suggestion.

"Yeah, Larry, I guess you're right," I mumbled, getting up from my chair anxious to be on my way. I didn't want to show the mounting embarrassment I felt flooding my cheeks. It would give my feelings away. I wasn't one to show my emotions.

Driving off to the construction job I still held, Larry's words remained an unanswered challenge to my mind. "You know that boy has got something, at that," I meditated. "All those things I was taught as a child and here I've never been saved myself."

Yet, something inside of me wanted to argue. "But you've been going to the altar and praying," it suggested.

More powerful words came though saying, "But a person knows the moment he is born again into the kingdom of God, and you know you aren't."

Pulling into the parking lot at work, I ended the argument. "All right then, tonight I'll get saved."

Well, I honestly tried that night. I bawled and boohooed at the altar. Naomi prayed with me awhile, then W.R. and Lamar took over. I wore them all out and left the services feeling empty and low. I earnestly craved reassurance. I needed salvation for the sickness in my soul. I desperately needed God's help in overcoming this growing craving for alcohol.

By the tenth night I finally wore myself out. Dejectedly, I

cried out to the Lord, "I can't do no more, God. I've tried and tried to be saved. Please accept me now 'cause I can't do no more."

Then it happened. A peace descended upon me and a feeling of great contentment flooded my body. That was all it took. The moment I knew I couldn't save myself God stepped in. Total, complete surrender is what it took.

I finally understood a Scripture I had heard many times—"By grace are you saved, through faith. It is the *gift* of God, *not of works* lest any man should boast."

Tears of joy streamed down my face. For the first time, I realized I was now a child of God.

I was smiling to myself now as I leaned forward in my easy chair. Those memories of the past few years had been pleasant. I was happy in spirit and in finally realizing my childhood dream to sing gospel music.

"Naomi, listen, here's my idea," I suggested. 'With the popularity of this song now, everybody's gonna hear it. We're pretty well-known already. The demand for us to sing is growing. In fact with us still working, we can't even meet those demands. Maybe we should go full time.

"It's an exciting prospect," she agreed.

"Let's call the others and see what they say."

With the exception of Dempsey Rainwater, everybody agreed that now was the time to go full time. Dempsey's departure required some shifting of vocal parts. Lamar volunteered to sing bass, so I switched to baritone with Naomi taking up my tenor. Since our songs were so high pitched, the transition was simple.

Our first engagement after going full time presented some unforgettable moments. It was a week-long revival in a small Nazarene church in Pioneer, Ohio. As usual we were having transportation problems.

Jim Kirkland from Douglas, Georgia, had recently joined us as our first full-time pianist. He wasn't acquainted with such problems. "Whose car are we going in?" he asked.

"Yours," I responded quickly.

Jim didn't act too happy about that as the bunch of us, plus luggage and equipment, filled his car to capacity and more. Protests aside, we headed northward.

The weather made our trip even more interesting. We had left the milder climate of Georgia, made our way through Tennessee and Kentucky into the hitherto unfamiliar environs of Ohio. When we arrived, there were two feet of snow on the ground. Dressed in our light Georgia clothes, we about froze to death.

We were soon warmed by the response of the people. Night after night, the church packed out with people wanting to hear the gospel in song. It was thrilling to look into the sea of shining faces, many with tears streaming down.

W.R., Lamar, Naomi and myself stood close to an old battered, upright piano. Jim hammered away at the keyboard producing melodious sounds that seemed impossible coming from such a hand-me-down instrument. People came to the altar each night sobbing their way to a life of victory.

Eli Lipps, the preacher, was blind. He seemed like one of the prophets walking off the pages of the Old Testament. Each night he interrupted our singing with an unforgettable appeal to the congregation.

He groped his way to the familiar platform, rested his hands on the pulpit while feeling its hardened surface. Then he turned his sightless eyes toward heaven, as if able to view something unseen with a perfect vision, and began praying.

His voice rose in a magnificent crescendo of volume and intensity. Like a giant tidal wave rushing before an erupting volcano, he soared to oratorical heights, crashing down on accented words and blasting off to new elevations of verbal splendor.

I can still hear him—"Oh, God, we approach you on behalf of these folks. We got Sister Naomi here and Brother James and they've got two children at home. We got Brother Lamar here, he's got five children. Lord, think about Brother W.R. and his six children. Oh, God, we appeal to you now. Oh, God, we're looking for you to move. Oh, God, we're standing in need. Hear us tonight, Oh, Lord. We wait on you, dear God."

The unique prayer he prayed was repeated nightly. Afterwards the people gave generously. But most of all, they got saved. It was a thrilling start to our step in faith. A new life was ahead for all of us.

*James, son of a
Holy Roller.*

*1946–the first quartet. Charlie Norris, Jr., Lamar, W.R., James, and
Mrs. Charlie Norris, Sr., pianist.*

Naomi at age sixteen.

*James, Naomi,
and Carlton–1951.*

1967—the group as it appeared on a Nashville television special.

Segos on "PTL Club."

The group today, and the Silver Eagle.

Sego Brothers and Naomi—(left to right) W.R., Ronnie, James, Naomi, Doug Green, Eddie Boland.

The Segos plus grandchildren Dawn Renee Sego and Jim Sego, and Dolly Parton.

NINE

Deceived!

Somewhere along the way, I got the idea that God had given the group a special anointing to be ambassadors to the whole world. I realized we were in great demand. The records were selling. We had become an overnight success after fourteen years.

Pride dangerously filled my heart.

I became particularly elated when approached by a representative of a large flour-milling company who offered to sponsor a television show just for us. What a break! We would be seen all over the South on the weekly program.

W.R., Lamar, Jim, Naomi and myself sat down in the living room of our house one day to discuss the program. I could see everybody was in a dream world as we talked about the format for the proposed TV program.

The telephone interrupted our discussion. It was a promoter who had booked us regularly. "I called to tell you about some real big news," he explained.

I couldn't think of anything bigger than the offer we had from the flour-milling company but I said, "Go ahead, I'm listening."

"James, I've just had the opportunity to buy out one of the South's largest singing promoters. Part of the agreement is that I'm to take over all the group he's been promoting in gospel singing. With the other groups I have, this has opened the door for me to do a nationwide gospel singing show."

"Well, that's just great," I responded in genuine congratulations. "I'm really glad for you."

"That's not all, James," he said. "I want The Sego Brothers and Naomi to be one of the show's regulars. This would be great for both of us."

"Wow. That is great. What an opportunity. But, wait—" I gulped, remembering the lucrative offer we had just received from the flour company.

"What's up?" he asked.

"Man, I can't. I'm sorry. I'm committed to do another television show with somebody else. We just received an offer from a sponsor for our own television show."

"James," he implored, "you've got to tell them no. Tell them you changed your mind. Tell them you're not available. Just tell them something. This is a much better opportunity for you. You'll receive coast-to-coast exposure. It'll bring you better bookings with larger audiences and higher ratings."

Then appealing to my good business sense, he added, "Not to mention the fact you'll be able to demand a fatter wad of that green folding stuff wherever you appear in concert."

He spent the better part of an hour trying to convince me that the best decision to make would be to cast my lot with him. All that he offered certainly sounded appealing to me. By the time the phone conversation had ended, he had fully convinced me to forget the other offer and sign with him.

Several weeks passed. We practiced our songs to perfection so we would be ready to begin production soon. One evening after the group had left following a practice session and our children had been put to bed, Naomi and I relaxed over a late cup of coffee. The new opportunities that lay ahead seemed to be our constant conversation piece.

The telephone rang interrupting our sand castle-building. "Just sit still, honey," I said, hastening across the room before its ringing awakened the children, "I'll get it."

"Hello."

"Hey, James, guess who?"

"Well, how are you doing, brother?" I asked delightedly upon recognizing the voice. It was Sam Smith, a booking agent who handled gospel groups. "I haven't seen you in a mighty long time."

"Yeah, I've been pretty busy," he allowed.

"What can I do for you?"

"Listen, I've been doing some changes in scheduling groups on my program and I'd sure like to use you and your group."

My pride was inflated. "Wow, three different sources and they all want us for television," I thought. "How good can you get?"

"I'd sure like to help you 'cause you're such a good friend," I replied, "but it's like this, I can't. I'm already scheduled for the 'Gospel Singing Hour,' and it's going to be starting soon."

There seemed to be a long silence at the other end of the line. "James, I hate to be the one to tell you this," he said softly. "Maybe you don't even know. But if you're on that program, you'd better leave for Nashville right now. Maybe you misunderstood or something but they started taping that show today."

"But that can't be," I said, bewildered. "The show's producer told me plain I was on it. Why, I even canceled my other sponsor." It suddenly occurred to me I had been deceived. "You mean this guy is now telling me to go fly a kite?"

I asked bitterly.

"I don't know about all that, James," he answered. "Look, I'm sorry to have been the one to tell you this. Maybe you'd better call this guy and find out what's going on."

My voice must have risen several decibels. Recognizing from experience the note of anger it held, Naomi crept close to my side tugging on my arm, trying to listen to the other end of the conversation.

I hung up the phone and sat staring at it. "What is it, honey?" she asked softly.

My hands shook as she reached for them. I jerked them away impatiently and scratched my head. My throat felt dry, parched. "Boy, I could use a drink," I thought to myself. "No, no, I can't allow myself to even consider that."

I tried to stay calm, briefly explaining the situation to Naomi. "It looks like we've been deceived by this promoter," I said dejectedly.

"Before you get more upset, call him," she advised. "Maybe there's a reason. It could be a misunderstanding. Maybe we're not on the first show they're filming."

"Okay," I agreed. "Maybe you're right." Naomi's words had a soothing effect on me.

I went back to the telephone. Finally the operator got through to a place in Nashville and after much persuasion I managed to get the "Gospel Singing Hour" producer on the phone. "Listen, I understand you're taping the show already," I said, trying to keep my voice under control. "What does all this mean?"

"I'm sorry, James, to have to tell you." Impatience showed in his voice. "I've been putting it off. Yes, it's true. We are taping the show now."

"Look, you made a promise to me and I even canceled my other show on your advice," I told him emphatically. All the while I was getting madder.

"Okay, James, if you want the truth, this is it," he said bluntly. "I know you used to be bad to drink and, frankly, I think this would be a bad image for the show."

His words plunged like a dagger into my heart. A rage flooded inside of me. Nearly a minute passed before I could trust myself to speak again.

"But," I retorted, "since the Lord answered my prayers, I haven't been drinking. I haven't had a drink in nearly three years. You going to hold that against me? What am I supposed to do with my other sponsor? I've already canceled him."

"I'm sorry, I don't know," he replied stiffly. "Maybe you can work something else out with them."

Slamming the receiver down on its cradle, I leaned wearily against the living room wall. My thoughts were befuddled. "I don't understand this, Naomi," I said. "I've put a lot of confidence in that show's producer. But he's sold me out. Why didn't he talk to me about this before? I had no idea a brother would do this to you. What in the world are we gonna do now? We turned two others down and then we finally get cut out ourselves."

"James, I don't know," she answered softly. "I don't have any answers. I just know we can't put our confidence in man. We have to place it with God. But you can't let this get you down. Let's pray about it."

I looked at the concern etched in her face. "I can't," I whined. "I can't. I gotta get out of here and think."

Naomi shook her head. "Now James, don't go and do something foolish."

I ran for the closet to get my jacket, ignoring Naomi's pleading. I left her standing in the open door and ran down the steps to the car. I drove off furiously. Tires squealing. Temper boiling.

I was crushed. I drove around Macon not seeing the people and places I passed. They all went by in a blur. The next thing I knew I was standing at the counter of some unknown liquor store buying a bottle.

Clutching the brown sack with its contents, I hopped into the car and drove near the Ocmulgee River on the outskirts of the city. Maybe I could drink and think while watching the river.

"I can't believe a situation like this could happen to me as long as I've known this guy," I muttered. I drank and drowned myself in self-pity. "I can't believe this," I repeated to myself. "I've known this guy for years."

I didn't want to blame the people who had taken our place on the telecast. They were great Christian folks and I liked them. But self-pity continued to eat at me.

"Why," I said to myself, "they even come from the same neck of the woods I come from. They wouldn't even be on that show if we hadn't helped boost them."

I sat there alone looking at the stars twinkling against the black velvet sky. I wondered how God in His great universe could have allowed this to happen to me.

"Well, it's a shabby way to treat somebody who has worked with you for all those years," I muttered to myself as consciousness slipped away. Before I knew it, I had passed out.

Naomi was sick with worry when I didn't return shortly. She had no way of knowing that I had broken my years of abstinence from the bottle. Little did I realize what getting drunk this time would mean.

TEN

A Helpless Gospel Singing Drunk

In the early hours of the morning I awoke from a cramped position in the front seat of the car. Rubbing my hot-lidded eyes I stretched my arms to ease the tension created from their cramped position, reached out and turned on the ignition. It was still dark. A low morning fog lay over the river.

I drove towards home, not considering I could be arrested for driving while intoxicated. I stopped for another bottle at a bar I passed on the way home. I wanted to continue drowning my sorrows and escaping thoughts that continually crowded into my mind. I arrived home and let myself in.

"James, is that you?" a voice startled me as it spoke out of the darkness of the living room. It was Naomi.

"Yeah, ish me." I hoped she wouldn't notice the slurred speech, but she did.

She switched on the living room light and took a look at my disheveled appearance. "Oh, James, what have you done to yourself?" she cried, dropping to her knees sobbing.

Through the fog of my drunken stupor, I realized she was praying for me. I was moved by her empathy and my eyes grew misty as she prayed, but I still uncorked the bottle and took a long swig before staggering down the hall to bed.

Slits of sunlight pierced the venetian blinds stabbing my eyelids. My head throbbed. My body ached. The familiar sounds of Naomi talking to the children in another room made me conscious of my surroundings. My dulled senses began returning ever so slightly.

I wanted release from the painful memories that were returning, too. I groped about for the bottle and found it with trembling hands.

"Just one small drink to get me through this morning," I thought. "That's all. I'll quit. It'll be like medicine for my shakes." I lifted the bottle and gulped down the fiery drink that jerked me upright as it hit my empty stomach.

I shoved aside the covers and sat up, putting one foot slowly on the floor, then another. I arose cautiously testing the ability of my feet and legs to hold me upright. The room spinned.

Stumbling into the bathroom, I held onto the lavatory and glared in the mirror. I was astonished at the visage reflecting back at me. The man was a stranger. He was not the man I wanted to be. His bloodshot eyes had a sad, hopeless stare. He wasn't the clear-eyed, happy-go-lucky gospel singer I'd tried so hard to become.

I jerked at my clothes impatiently popping several buttons in the process. Maybe a shower would restore my morale.

While showering, the hot steam penetrating my whiskey-soaked skin, Naomi tapped lightly at the bathroom door. "James, are you all right? I heard you get up. Can you eat something?"

Naomi was always the same. Gentle. Loving. Ashamed of my treatment of her, I said patiently, "No thanks, I'll just have some black coffee."

In a few short months, I traded in my appetite for incipient alcoholism. Drinking provided me with a quick and easy mood changer. I continually used it as a crutch when self-pity or anger overwhelmed me. The singing engagements continued to come, and for a while I was able to stay sober during our engagements. I could drink a couple of beers, a half pint or even a full pint of whiskey, and still go about my business. Never once did I think that this constant drinking would be my downfall.

While dressing to leave for a performance one evening, I overheard Naomi. Her voice was barely audible as it drifted through the partially opened door of our bedroom. She was filled with increasing concern.

"I wish James would talk about the situation," she was confiding to W.R. and Lamar who had come by the house early. "Maybe then he could face this problem. He just keeps everything inside and lets it eat at him. He won't even let me bring up the subject. He's just got to get over this soon before it damages his health permanently."

Naomi's words troubled me. But I didn't stop drinking.

I might have beaten my drinking problems if another event hadn't occurred causing me to fall into an even greater depression. Mama passed away. For years she had suffered from a combination of serious ailments including heart trouble and diabetes. But I always relied on her. She had an inner strength that motivated me.

Some people might have called mama headstrong and dominating but she had a deep compassion for people in need. She walked closely with God. During the late fifties when I was struggling along building houses during the week and singing on the weekend, I'd be down to my last few dollars frequently. Many times I was flat broke. Mama always had the answer to just such problems. "I tell you what we'll do. Let's pray. That's the only answer." And from there, we'd begin what she called "a season of prayer." That meant getting down on your knees in prayer for about two hours.

Never once did the Lord ever fail to answer those prayers. I'd get calls in November and December from people who suddenly decided they wanted me to build something for them. It was the wrong season to be building but that didn't stop us. Daddy and my two brothers joined in frequently on the jobs. I saw that God was real and He actually cared what happened to people by answering those prayers. We never went hungry.

Mama had a unique way of cheering me up. If she ever heard me talking negatively or looking depressed, she was quick to respond. "No, son, don't ever talk or act that way. Let's get our minds straight. By the help and grace of God, things are gonna be all right. Things are gonna get better."

Her optimism always stirred me. Once she got me smiling, she'd laugh. "Now you've got the picture," she'd say, "things are getting better all the time. Lord help me, they are."

"Now here's one lady I could always count on," I cried softly at her funeral. "What am I going to do without her?"

Somehow I managed to stay sober for the funeral even though I wanted to drown my sorrows in drink. I felt I owed mama that decency.

Standing beside the flower-covered, open coffin where mama lay, I remembered the years of deceit when I continually tried to keep my drinking from her. The only thing I'd ever told her about were those first few teen-age drinking sprees. She knew drinking had run a devastating course on both sides of the family, Erskines and Segos. She fearfully tried to impress me with this. She knew an alcoholic spirit could be passed down from other generations to me. Had it already grabbed control of my life?

Until the most recent setback over the television program, I had managed to keep my drinking limited to an occasional night on the town with buddies. That didn't seem to satisfy anymore. My burdens now were more than I felt I could stand. I couldn't find comfort or solace anywhere. At least drinking temporarily allowed me to escape.

I stared at daddy standing by the coffin. His lips were moving. I knew he was talking to mama as if she could hear him. They had been together forty-nine years. I knew daddy never visualized them apart. It tore me emotionally to see him so forlorn. The strain of losing mama seemed to age him ten years overnight.

I glanced again at mama. I could hear again what she'd told me a few days before she died. I had gone by their house for a brief visit. She lay immobile. Her wrinkled skin as white as the sheet covering her frail body. Her silver hair damp and tousled by the countless days of being bedridden.

But her smile was gentle and sweet as I took her hand and said, "Mama, maybe we'd better not leave for this all night sing in Nashville. Maybe we ought to stay here with you."

She patted my hand feebly. "No, son," she replied. "You go on. Sing and tell them the Lord is coming soon. Don't worry about me. If I die before you get back, you'll know where to find me."

I left mama's house in a strange mood. When I got home words to a song began coming to me. A paper sack was the only thing I could find to write on. In pencil I scribbled these words.

When cares of this life are laid down,
I'll go to receive my shining crown;
I'll see the precious One who died for me,

And then I know I'll really be free.
I've worked so hard for my Lord,
I've sung and preached His holy Word;

Though Satan tried so hard to stop me,
But when I get to heaven, I'll be free.

The hardships I've endured now seem so small,
Sometimes I've been tempted, but didn't fall;
I know you're still my hope eternally,
And when I get to heaven, I'll be free.
I got news of her death when we phoned home from a truck
stop on the way back from the concert. Like the song, mama
could say, "I'll Really Be Free." She was ready—I wasn't.

Daddy was sobbing uncontrollably as several family
members led him away from the coffin. His sobs snapped me
back to my surroundings. The grief lay upon my heart like a
heavy weight.

I was drunk for days after the funeral. Naomi constantly
pleaded with me to "please quit." She'd lay awake each night
when I failed to return home trying to pray. Sometimes she
worried that I would never return home alive. Each time the
phone rang, fear raced through her veins like ice water. She
dreaded the thought of hearing a voice on the phone telling her
my life had been snuffed out in a tragic accident. All of which
was possible since I was living on the edge of disaster.

Countless times she wept over me when she couldn't revive
me following a night of drinking. I frequently blacked out even
after sobering up. My only response to Naomi would be to
leave the house as soon as I got up. Then I began the day's
search for the first drink. I had a horror of not being able to get a
drink when I needed one.

Other singing groups heard about my problem and promised
to pray for my condition. But instead, many of them ended up
talking to each other about me. At first, the groups had gone
along with the story I was sick. In reality, I was.

Then one night we appeared at an all night sing held at a

baseball park in a south Georgia town. Our bus was being repaired so we were traveling by car. W.R. was opening the trunk of the car when the promoter walked up.

"I'm sorry, boy," he said, "but we can't let your group perform here tonight."

Why?" demanded W.R.

"I'd really like to let you," he admitted, "but the other groups have refused to appear if I allow you to sing. So you see, I don't really have a choice. I'm sure you understand."

I wasn't actually drunk that particular night. "I could have performed," I insisted when W.R. brought the story to me. I remembered the many times before when I had gone on stage. Just before stepping into the spotlight, I would straighten up, draw my shoulders back, thrust out my chin and walk out smiling. Then, I'd sing my heart out.

No matter what my physical condition was, I gave myself completely to an audience. I was in perfect control of my voice, my body and every movement I made.

Some hidden power transformed me on stage giving me the appearance of being sober and allowing me to do the things I loved the most—sing the gospel. Somehow the drive I had for singing allowed me to get through the concerts. No matter how my knees shook. No matter how dry my throat felt or how my head throbbed. It all left when I performed.

My heart was broken when W.R. finished telling me of the promoter's decision. Guilt bore down upon me. "I've done blown it," I admitted, "and caused everybody else to suffer too."

We had taken a motel room for the night but with the sudden change in plans we checked out. I flopped on the back seat of the car as we rolled down the road without a destination.

We were nearly broke this time. No other concerts were scheduled for a week. The car was silent. The tires whined along the blacktop. Everybody seemed afraid to speak their feelings. "The sad thing," I thought to myself, "is some of those who rejected me are doing things as bad as drinking. Why pick on me?"

But things didn't get better. They grew worse.

I finally got to the place I was unable to perform. I grew weaker and sicker as alcohol took its toll in my body. The group still toured performing with the pianist singing my harmony part. I'd lay drunk on the bus listening only to whatever music flowed through my imagination. Naomi lived in constant dread that I would wake up, get off the bus and come staggering into the building where they were singing. It was a fear that could have happened, but never did.

W.R. and Lamar became frustrated in attempts to make me realize what I was doing. They tried talking sensibly. They tried shaming me. They challenged me to be a man and lay aside the drinking. None of it worked. I only whined and begged their forgiveness.

A trip to North Carolina was near. Concerts. Churches. All night sings. W.R. and Lamar had grown so disgusted they refused to make the trip. Honestly, I couldn't have blamed them.

But Naomi was the real trouper. She recognized God had called her to sing and she stayed true to that calling come what may. For several nights, it was just "and Naomi" when only the pianist accompanied her.

People who knew the situation often asked, "Why haven't you given up?"

"This is what I must do," she always replied. "The Lord has given me talent. I've never even thought about quitting. Oh, sure, many times I have felt more like crying than singing, but a power has always sustained me until the performance was over."

All the while I grew more bitter toward the promoter and a few individuals I felt sold us out. Hate began to grow inside of me. Something demanded revenge. But I still sensed the Spirit of the Lord striving within me.

That gentle, unseen power prevented me from surrendering totally to the forces of evil, forces driving me into some foolish act of vindication. Roots of bitterness were so securely entwined about my heart, it would be a long time before I could be free from the clutches of its tentacles.

ELEVEN

"I Am Going to Heal You"

Drink had so wasted my body in those several months that I became completely bedridden. Many times Naomi prepared a meal for me and I simply could not eat. I had no appetite for food, yet my whole body screamed for alcohol.

At times I pleaded tearfully with Naomi, "Honey, get me a drink. Ple-ea-se? I've got to have a drink now."

She looked at me hopelessly, wondering how I had allowed myself to sink into such a pitiful condition. She asked herself frequently, "Will James ever recover?" Often she walked over to my bed, knelt down, buried her face in her hands, and sobbed and prayed.

I never understood how Naomi could have been so patient. Yet she never grumbled or complained. All the while as my health declined, the bills mounted. My drinking habit had taken a bigger and bigger bite out of our income.

As for me, I had lost all sense of caring. Just getting relief for the thirst raging within me was all that mattered.

"Just one more drink, please, Naomi, then I'll quit," I continually told her. "I promise you, honey. I really mean it this time."

My inebriated mind never thought beyond the next drink. Naomi frequently gave in to my begging. She realized that although it was destroying me, alcohol was at least a source of temporary relief for my craving. Without it, she was convinced I would have died.

Many times she played the masquerade. Donning an overcoat, scarf and dark glasses, she would drive to a liquor store where she purchased the hated but needed whiskey. She knew it momentarily dispelled my physical agony and cooled my feverish brain. She carefully avoided buying whiskey more than once or twice in the same place for fear of being recognized. That would have made matters even worse.

W.R. and Lamar begged her to put me in a hospital. Knowing my supply would be cut off, I refused to go. But as time passed and my condition worsened, Naomi surrendered to my brothers' insistent urging and admitted me to the White Cross Hospital in Atlanta.

That was just the first of many alcoholic hospitals for me. In a couple years' time, I was in and out of several—just to "dry out." I always felt great for a short while once the drying out process was over. But that thirst for whiskey seemed to stick with me. And once out of the hospital when the thirst struck, I tried to satisfy it.

In late 1964, I entered the Peachtree Clinic in Atlanta. The place had gained notoriety of a sort because of the numerous show business personalities who had been treated successfully there. Its success rate was greatly challenged by my drinking problems.

The usual battery of tests were conducted. One nurse inserted a needle putting medicine in. Another followed with a needle drawing blood out. Everywhere I turned nurses were shoving small white cups at me. "Drink this," one nurse said, while another directed, "give me a specimen." It was give-and-take all day. I endured the routine with a helpless indifference. I was too sick to care.

Finally the last test was taken. The information compiled. Lying in bed, I stared blankly at the ceiling. It was speckled rough by a paint brush. I had done many ceilings like that in times past working with daddy.

Outside the door, I heard my doctor's voice. He was giving instructions to a nurse. Somehow he always seemed in a hurry whenever he made his rounds. He never wasted words, never lingered. His greeting was cut-and-dried, thoroughly professional. Looking at the chart at the foot of my bed, he fondled his stethoscope as he compared information on his clipboard with the chart.

"Sego, I believe you want me to be truthful with you," he said, making a notation on the chart. "We have evaluated the data from your examination and frankly the results are not good. There is every indication that you will never live to be forty years old."

"I won't live to be forty?" I stammered. A chill of apprehension ran through me. His words were stark, foreboding. "But doctor, why—?"

"Your liver is terribly swollen and functioning at only 26 percent of its capacity. Sego, if you don't quit drinking, it will kill you very soon."

Then he walked away.

I left the hospital determined to quit. But the hate and bitterness I harbored never left me. It festered—fueled by constant rumors about me and the group. Anybody connected with gospel music knew I was a drunk. The group's reputation suffered. Many times they were treated poorly because of me. That only made me more bitter. Before long my condition regressed to where I was due for readmission to dry out.

Early one morning, I awoke with the shakes. My body ached. I realized Naomi and my brothers would be back that morning from a tour. I wanted to come down off a drunk before they walked in—yet every nerve demanded relief. I had been left home with Claudell. She had moved in with us in an attempt to care for me. Most of the time though she simply gave in to my whims.

I felt sorry for myself. I couldn't travel anymore doing the thing I loved the most. More and more I had been telling the group to go ahead without me. I didn't want to be responsible for holding them back. Yet in countless ways, I knew I was.

The sounds of doors opening and closing and voices filling the house signaled the group's return. In a few minutes, Naomi was in my room. Dismayed at my appearance, she began crying. "James, when are you ever going to quit drinking?" she asked. "It's going to kill you."

"I know . . . I know," I whispered weakly. "But could I have just one little drink . . . I just gotta." Suddenly I became enraged. I reached down for a bedroom shoe and flung it at the small dog following Naomi.

"What's wrong with you, James?" she questioned as the frightened dog ran yelping from the room. Its stub of a tail tucked tightly against its backside.

"That ugly dog, I can't stand him," I shouted as I fell back trembling on my pillow. A rage flew over me.

Naomi looked at me strangely.

"He just stares at me all day," I said bitterly. "He just about drives me up a wall. Why does he have to stare at me all the time?"

The dog was a small bulldog puppy I had bought several weeks before for my youngest boy, Ronnie. It was a case of love at first sight when Ronnie saw the dog. Since I was home most of the time though, the dog grew attached to me.

My frayed nerves were causing frequent emotional upsets. There were others. But for the most part, my upsets centered on the dog. I felt like he was always sneaking up on me. I grew constantly agitated when I saw his bulging black eyes staring at me from across the room. Several times before, I had thrown objects at the mutt. All I succeeded in doing was creating a mess in the room.

Naomi realized I was near the breaking point. "James, it's not the dog's fault," she reasoned. "Please let me take you back to the hospital. You need help if you're this nervous."

"Aw . . . it wouldn't do any good, Naomi."

"Please, maybe this time it will. Let's go before you get too sick again."

Somehow I realized the terrible pressure I had placed on Naomi. She looked strained and tired. Reluctantly, I consented and arrangements were hurriedly made.

On arrival, I was met by a wheelchair-pushing nurse in the lobby. She maneuvered me to a room and gave the usual rundown of what to expect during the next several days. I could have quoted it verbatim for her.

"You'll be given liquor anytime you want it. Some vitamin B will be given daily for your nerves. Please see that you're faithful in taking them. We also have a schedule of lectures planned for you to attend. Remember, we're all your friends here. You won't be allowed to have any visitors unless you choose to do so. Your name will also remain anonymous to other patients. Are there any questions?"

I listened to the ritual patiently. I had heard it many times before. "Oh, I reckon I'll do okay," I mumbled. "This isn't my first time here. I know what to do."

"Nevertheless," the nurse replied gently, "we're here to help you understand your problem and overcome it. We'll simply need your help too. I hope we can count on it."

"Yeah, I'll cooperate," I allowed. "It looks like I don't have any other real choice."

Several days passed uneventfully. Then, the d.t.'s started. The hallucinations of the bulldogs and snakes followed. But through it, I realized I had been living a nightmare for years. Something was controlling me—destroying my mind and body. I couldn't let it continue. I had to stop.

Slowly I began the road back. I was motivated by the hallucinations. They had scared the wits out of me. The hospital, one of the best in the nation, also helped in drying me out and getting me on a balanced diet. Mrs. Snow, an elderly nurse with sharp features, bright blue eyes and a soft touch, was in charge of my wing. She had seen me coming and going at the hospital. Somehow she took a personal interest—an interest reminiscent of mama.

"I mean business this time," I announced when she walked into my room. "I've really come to the end of my road."

"If that's what you want, James," she responded, "you can have it. But you're the person who decides that—not me."

"I really want help. I've got to change."

"Alcohol is killing you," she said. "That's plain to see."

"I know it is, yet I keep drinking. It seems like the first drink is stimulating for a while but then it dies on you. The only thing you can jack it back up with is another drink. Then another, and another. The next thing you know you're drunk."

I guess this time I had gotten desperate enough to follow Mrs. Snow's orders. She had the right combination of tenderness and toughness—like mama—to deal with me. She loved me, made me eat properly and helped me get my strength back. I'm sure she must have been praying for me all the while too. Many people were.

Under Mrs. Snow's watchful eye, my body began responding immediately. I began to feel as if I had the problem licked. Before long, I was released and strong enough to begin traveling again with the group. Boy, was I ever glad to be back singing. Many times that desire was the sole thing that kept me alive.

I tried making friends with folks and renewing friendships that had long been neglected on the circuit. There was little success. I detected hesitance and mistrust from most people. Some groups openly shunned any association with me. The word was out. Even a few promoters boycotted us at singings. Probably rightly so, since nobody—me included—knew when I might start another binge.

Naomi and my brothers often wondered if we would ever gain people's confidence again. But I asked myself the opposite question. "Would I ever have confidence in people?" I didn't know the answer.

Russell Sims, a friend from the past, showed up in Macon one day. It just happened to be one of the days I was depressed. "You can't trust anyone," I grumbled. Of course, I excluded Naomi from the accusation. She always stood by.

"James, I don't know why I'm here," Russell explained. "I felt like the Lord wanted me to come, so here I am. I'm prepared to make you an offer. I want you to join my record company and do an album for me."

I laughed in his face. "Yeah," I replied sarcastically, "I know all about people who make promises about wanting to draw up contracts with me."

"I thought you might think that way, James." He paused and reached into a briefcase he was carrying. "So I brought some proof. Now, here are the contracts ready for your signature and here's a cashier's check. Now will you go to Nashville and do that album?"

My heart softened as the tentacles of bitterness loosened their hold. Even so, I was so proud I held back making any comment. I looked across the room at Naomi. She sat with fingers crossed wanting me to conquer my hate and make a new start.

"Okay," I finally responded, "I'll do it." Naomi literally danced across the floor to hug me.

Later we went to Nashville and recorded the album for Russell's company. Russell was good for me. Through his actions, I began to trust people. It was clear that God had directed him to us. He also seemed to understand my problem. He knew alcoholism was a sickness, a sickness God could heal. In the process, God used him to restore my faith in people.

But early in 1966, guilt began eating away at me for letting Naomi and my brothers down so many times. I had put them through considerable shame because of my drinking. Somehow I couldn't bury the past—and leave it there. Physically, I had over extended myself in traveling. I had taxed my body trying to make up for lost time. In the process, my nerves frayed again to the breaking point.

We stopped at a restaurant one day on tour. I found myself seated near somebody who had too much to drink. The scent of booze wafted through the air. Something ran through me.

"No," I thought to myself, "not this time. I've made it now. I'm not going back."

But the temptation rode home with me, tantalizing my taste buds. I soon found an excuse to leave the house for a walk. "I've got to stop," I told myself to no avail.

I passed a bar. The aroma of beer reached my nostrils. I knew it wasn't going to be easy. By the time I was a block past the bar, I felt I had the battle won. The further I walked the more I thought about how good a glass of cold beer would be. I imagined it in my mind—the sudsy froth trickling down the sides of a glass. I felt the little streams of golden brew running down my parched throat. I felt its tingling sensation in my mouth. My imagination began to run wild. I saw myself downing one beer after another. The more I drank the more I wanted. One after another. My senses whirled.

"I can't stand it," I screamed. I turned and ran back to the bar where I soon lost count. Whiskey followed beer. One drink after another—just like I saw. I finally reached capacity. My vessel overflowed.

Staggering home in the wee hours of the morning, I flung myself on an empty bed. When Naomi walked in the next morning to tell me Russell was there, she knew what had happened. A whiskey bottle lay empty on the floor. The smell of vomit and stale whiskey hung over me. My clothes were rumpled, my hair matted.

"You're drunk," she cried in disgust.

"I need help," I slurred.

I arose weaving on my pin-like legs and staggered toward her. I had just enough sense to realize I had finally come to the end of the road. I reached for her hands patting them gently.

"Naomi, thisch ish it," I spoke with slurred sobs. "Thisch ish about ash far ash I can, hic, go. If I don'ta get shome help, I'm not gonna make it." My voice trailed off. I blacked out.

Russell had a friend who was director of a Seventh Day Adventist Hospital in Madison, Tennessee. They managed to get me admitted as an emergency case.

A week later I awoke in my room. Thoughts of my last drunk rushed my mind. I remembered crying out, "Lord, please, please, forgive me of all my sins," before I passed out.

God. My thoughts turned back to God.

I looked around the room. I knew I was alone and in another alcoholic hospital. There was no mistake about that. A sense of shame overwhelmed me. I was back.

I prayed endlessly. "Lord, please forgive me. Take over my life. Not only do I want to sing for you but I want to live for you.

I can't go on any more like this. Please help me. Please."

My eyes brimmed over. As I prayed I felt a heavy burden slip from my shoulders as if a lead coat had been removed. A strange sense of calm overcame me. I looked about me. A warm glow spread softly across the room. Its light seemed alive. It moved until it seemed to be standing beside the bed.

The beat of my heart seemed to change as the light overshadowed me. The bitter roots of hate and hurt unwound and slipped away. Peace permeated the core of my being filling my heart with love.

A holy atmosphere was upon the room. I felt enveloped in God's love. Inside I knew God had made me a new creature. My despair had finally caused me to reach out to God allowing Him to take over the reins of my innermost being. I had finally gotten desperate enough to ask God to change my life.

The glow of this presence grew intensely brighter. Its light was a brilliant amber color. I knew I was in the presence of a supernatural being. I believed it was He who would live forever.

I waited expectantly. Then I heard a voice saying audibly, "I am going to heal you."

The spoken words inspired me to sit up. I pushed aside the covers and sat on the side of the bed. I looked down at my legs. They were small and spindly—they didn't seem to belong to my body. A tingling started from my toes and began moving upward as new life rushed into them. Strength came into my legs.

The voice continued. "You must sing and praise me. I will be the captain of your life. Let the hate die in you now. It is a destructive force and is not of me."

And then the presence left as quickly as it had come. From that moment, I knew I was a changed man. I was a whole person. No longer was I bound to an insatiable appetite for alcohol. I was set free by the living presence who would henceforth control my life.

The next morning I was conscious and smiling. The hospital staff obviously thought my mind had snapped. A psychiatrist was dispatched to interview me.

"I want to talk with you," he announced, entering the room.

"No, I don't think so," I smiled. "I've already seen the man I need to talk with."

Unfazed by my reaction, the doctor sat and chatted with me for thirty minutes. "Well, I don't know what's happened to you," he said shaking his head, "but you're certainly different than the man who was admitted here a week ago. I don't see any reason why you can't be dismissed in a few days."

Several days passed. Finally I was permitted to call Naomi. "Honey, I'm ready to come home for good," I shouted when she answered the phone.

"Why, whatever do you mean, James?"

I told her about the miraculous visitation and how God had spoken to me. "Naomi, it's done. God has set me free."

"Praise the Lord! Is this really you, James?"

"It's the new me, Naomi."

"I'll be right there. I can hardly wait."

Back in the room, I leaned back on the bed and let my thoughts wander. I realized I had been a failure so many times simply trying to do things my own way. Now I could safely trust God with my life. After all He had kept me alive through this whole ordeal. For the first time I could understand that the devil had been trying to destroy me for years. "Why didn't I just surrender to the Lord before?" I wondered to myself.

My mind traced over the past few years settling on another event when the devil had almost taken my life. I had been visiting mama who was ill. Blondean, who was a registered nurse, was there caring for mama. It wasn't wise for me to be there since I had a terrible cold complete with fever, stuffy nose and aches. But I was concerned about mama and wanted to see her. I was also concerned I might not be able to perform in our next singing.

"Hey, Blondean," I was suddenly inspired. "Why don't you give me a shot of penicillin for my cold?"

"Can you take it?" she asked, knowing the hazards of a drug reaction.

"Sure, why do you ask?"

"Well, a drug reaction could produce a coma and death. Are you sure you're not allergic to it?"

"Naw," I replied, "I'm not allergic. I need something to get me out of this misery."

"Okay, roll up your sleeve," she instructed as she drew the antibiotic into a syringe.

Within several minutes of the injection, I blacked out. I awoke in the hospital with a team of nurses and doctors working over me. In my semi-conscious state, I heard a nurse say coldly, "Blood pressure, zero."

"Hey, I'm awake!" I wanted to tell them, but couldn't.

Another doctor walked in hurriedly and began giving instructions to the people working frantically over me. I still felt their hands on my body although I knew I was near death.

Hours later, I returned to consciousness. A doctor explained that Blondean had managed to reach him and describe what had happened with the penicillin. Until then, they had no idea how to treat me. I could have easily expired. Clinically, I had been dead.

But God had stepped in then, snatching me from the hands of the devil, and, now, He had healed me of alcoholism. I realized God had a purpose for me, a divine destiny. More than anything else, I wanted to sing and share the gospel. For the rest of my life, I determined Jesus Christ would be the captain of my ship. Sink or swim, I was with Him.

Naomi and I walked arm in arm from the hospital. We were both joyful. I took a long, final look at its imposing exterior as we drove away. I knew I would never again enter its doors.

The Sego Brothers and Naomi were once again a happy group of gospel singers. I told everyone I met about what the Lord had done for me. Some believed. Others doubted. I overheard many unkind comments—sometimes backstage, sometimes in the lobbies.

"So he's really saved now," some said. "Well, we'll see."

"Yeah" others agreed, "he'll go back to the bottle before long. Wait and see."

I didn't understand why people were so hypocritical. Couldn't a guy change? Yet I knew I had sowed seeds of suspicion and mistrust. Now I reaped the fruits of its harvest. "Time will prove it," I decided, "because God has done the work."

Frequently, I stood on the stage or behind a church pulpit and affirmed, "When the Lord does something, He does it well. He has delivered me from alcoholism. His healing touch has raised me up to declare that message, and His salvation is for everyone who will ask."

Lives were constantly changed. Drunks repented and found Christ. Sick bodies were healed. People developed new understanding of the horrors of alcohol. God was glorified.

TWELVE

Miracle of the Silver Eagle

Slumped in a worn seat of the old bus, I was soon lulled into a peaceful sleep. Noise from the big diesel engine roared in my ears. We had just finished a recording session in Nashville and were on our way back to Macon.

My rest was interrupted by Lamar's deep voice intruding into my dreamy state. "James, are you asleep?"

"Not now I ain't."

"Listen, I've come up with an idea."

"What is it?" I asked as I stretched, yawned and tried to bring my mind to attention.

"Look, why don't we move to Nashville?"

"Move to Nashville?" I responded.

"Yeah, I've been checking the appointment book," he gestured to our list of schedules that lay on his lap, "and we're spending nearly a third of our time singing in Nashville or somewhere around it."

The idea hit me with a shock of surprise. I wasn't too sure at the moment whether or not I wanted to pull up roots after twenty-five years of living in Macon. I had a lot of friends and relatives there. I was hesitant.

"Well, I'll give it some thought," I promised Lamar. "Right now I want to pick up that beautiful dream." I leaned back in the reclining seat and closed my eyes.

During the next week, the idea of moving occurred several times to me. "It might be a good idea from a business angle," I thought. "Banks in Macon do think small."

At various times we needed money to invest in recording session, bus repairs and other assorted needs. I had just recently gone to a local bank to arrange financing for a new bus. I explained to a friendly loan officer with a flower in his lapel how our old bus was not practical for the long trips our schedules now demanded.

He thought carefully and jotted down miscellaneous information. I never doubted he wouldn't consider the loan a good banking investment. Little did I realize he had no conception of the value of a bus.

"Okay, we'll do it like this," he suggested confidently. "We'll write up a mortgage on your cars plus two of your houses and I'll let you have $3,000."

"Three thousand dollars," I said, almost swallowing a dental plate.

"Yep, what do you say?" he asked.

I had no problem giving him an answer. Three thousand dollars was a mere drop in the bucket compared to the amount we needed. The Segos had already owned and paid for several buses. We had proven our credit was good. We'd have to put everything we owned on the line—almost to surrendering the clothes on our back—just to get a loan from this bank.

"Thanks, but that won't help," I said.

Driving home, I pondered the difference between banks in Macon and Nashville. I had borrowed $12,000 on a signature loan in Nashville for our last bus. The bank in "Music City,

U.S.A." recognized the strength of our record sales. Of course, dealing frequently with many gospel and country and western groups, bankers in Nashville understood the financing that accompanied the purchase of a bus. Bankers in Macon simply had no experience along these lines.

By the time I reached home, I had made up my mind to move. Naomi was home and I discussed the situation with her. She liked the idea of relocating. Only she wasn't thinking about financing buses. She had in mind putting several hundred miles between me and some of my old drinking buddies.

Several days passed before I had a chance to talk with Lamar again. "Hey, were you kidding about moving to Nashville?" I asked. "That's a pretty big step."

"Nope," he replied. "I still think it's a good idea."

"Well, let's get to work on it. I definitely think that's what we should do."

Making a special trip back to Nashville to look for property, I located a competent real estate man who showed us around town. We spent several days looking each section of town over. From West End Avenue to Nolensville Pike to Gallatin Pike to Clarksville Pike, we looked. Yet I couldn't find anything I wanted.

"Well, wait until tomorrow," he said cheerfully. "Maybe I'll have a place you'll be interested in."

The next day we drove north on U.S. Highway 31W. About eighteen miles from Nashville, we came to the tree-lined streets of a small town. I was immediately attracted by its clean appearance and homey atmosphere. "What town is this?" I questioned.

"White House, Tennessee," he answered. "Population, 500."

"Boy, this is a nice little town," I said.

"It's interesting," he suggested, "hardly any of the show

business people actually live in the city of Nashville. They usually live in some of the outlying suburbs like this or Hendersonville, Madison, Mt. Juliet and Franklin. If you buy a house around here, I think you'll be happy."

The agent showed us a new subdivision being built. Naomi and I fell in love with a beautiful ranch-type house on Cranor Drive. "Well, I'm ready to sign on the dotted line," I said, after looking the house over. "When I say I'm ready to do something, I do it! I'm ready to move in this minute."

"Great!" shouted the agent.

I bought one house in the subdivision and W.R. bought another one several blocks away. But after we all relocated, Lamar was the one who hesitated. He purchased a trailer and stayed there unhappily for about a year. Finally he left the group and moved back to Macon. For a while he went back to carpentry work.

In time, Lamar formed his own group with several of his talented children. His group, the Lamar Sego Family, has recorded several albums and done quite successfully in gospel singing.

R.C. Taylor from Nashville, Georgia, joined the group after Lamar left. Although we missed Lamar, we knew he was happy back in Macon.

Almost immediately we noticed the effect of moving to the Nashville area. People automatically sat up and took notice when the announcer said, "Here they are from Nashville, Tennessee—the Sego Brothers and Naomi." Being one of the three major recording centers of the country (the others: New York and Los Angeles), Nashville meant professional. I believe the group even improved with the move—as if, somehow, to fit the label of being from Nashville. The wisdom of the change was justified when our bookings and record sales began to soar.

Some of my relatives and friends in Georgia suggested I had

become highfalutin since moving to Nashville. One fellow even accused me of "belittling the state by moving." True, we had been named "Ambassadors of Good Will for Georgia" by Gov. Carl E. Sanders, and that title had been promoted extensively on the back of our album jackets. Perhaps it looked a little strange when Georgia's "Good Will Ambassadors" moved to Tennessee, but no harm was intended. We made the move simply believing it was the best for us.

The greater demand for bookings created the need for better transportation. Our first bus, a 1946 Flexible, was bought in 1960 with a loan of $2,500 from Rev. I.O. Allen, a Pentecostal preacher in Macon. It took another $2,500 just to make the bright blue Flexible roadworthy. Three engine overhauls later we had invested $9,000 more.

Traveling the highways and back roads of America has a way of wearing out gospel singers and buses. You never know when one or the other might break down. We rid ourselves of the Flexible and purchased two more buses, one from Talmadge Lewis and another from the Harvesters Quartet.

Tragedy still had a way of striking. At one time we had two buses with blown engines, and it was back to riding in cars for a short duration. "If I was ever gonna quit singing, it would be now," I thought several times.

But there was always saving grace in every situation. Talmadge Lewis replaced the engine on the bus we bought from him. We sold the other bus outright. Then, with cash and trade, we got a newer model General Motors 4104. During the next several years, we sunk $5,000 in the bus we dubbed the "workhorse." The bus was in excellent shape but it was still to small for extended trips.

Many opportunities had come our way. We were featured guests on several syndicated television programs based in Nashville. My heart's desire was satisfied. Television was bringing us into the homes of thousands of families across the land. Places I might not ever be able to visit. More opportunities opened for us to travel across country. Calls from California, Arizona, Texas. Some of the stops were a thousand miles apart. Several times we finished a Friday night program in Dallas and had to be in Indianapolis, Indiana, the next night. The "workhorse" couldn't make trips like that for long. I felt the pinch even more to get better transportation. Finally I went to a Nashville bank and got the approval to purchase another bus if I could come up with the down payment.

Filled with excitement, I could hardly wait and decided to fly out to Dallas and look over a place that specialized in buses. Soon after my arrival, I headed straight for the bus lot. I walked the length of the place, getting in and out of buses. Each time I felt disappointment overtaking me. The place was loaded with buses of various colors, sizes and shapes, but I couldn't find what I was looking for.

I turned to the bow-tie-clad salesman following me. By now, he had grown discouraged as one-by-one I had found fault with each bus he showed me. "Are these all the buses you got?" I questioned.

"Yeah," he replied, squinting in the sunshine, "this is it." Rather exasperated, he volunteered, "They've all got new engines. Everything is in tiptop shape. We'll give you a good guarantee."

I knew he was trying to press me for a sale. But I just couldn't get excited about anything I'd seen.

"Boss, I'm not trying to put your buses down or anything," I said, turning to him and trying to reflect my best "down home" manners, "but I believe I got a better bus than any of these back home."

About that time, a driver wheeled a new Silver Eagle bus

onto the lot. The hot Texas sun reflected off its shiny chrome bumpers and trim. A majestic sculpture of an eagle with its wings full spread, its head turned to the side, graced the front of the bus.

The luggage compartment doors were opened beneath the bus revealing a wealth of roomy storage. I saw clear through to the other side. The huge vehicle with its rear dual tandem wheels seemed like a giant eagle in a cage longing to be freed to soar down the open road.

As I looked it over, I felt like a child at Christmas time glimpsing through the window into a magic world of sugar plums and toys. I had to walk away lacking the means to satisfy my heart's desire.

The bus revved up my imagination. I saw us traveling in it down the open road. I heard the rhythmic hum of the big diesel engine and smelt its pungent fumes. I imagined feeling the cushiony ride of the giant air-filled shocks. How I longed for a bus like that!

"There ain't no way I'll ever have a bus like that," I thought. "I don't deserve nothing like that. I couldn't even pay for it if I had it." I shook my head trying to eject the idea from my thoughts, stuffed my hands in my pockets and walked away from the lot. There was nothing left to do but return home empty-handed.

On the flight back to Nashville, I couldn't get the Silver Eagle out of my mind. I remembered every detail of what the bus looked like. "It's no use," I admitted to myself.

I stared vacantly out the window of the plane. Fleecy white clouds flitted past catching my eyes. Still my thoughts were turned to the bus. I pictured myself walking all the way around it viewing the sleek motorcoach from every angle.

I leaned back in my seat trying to relax. A sleepiness had overcome most passengers as the flight roared eastward amid a tranquil atmosphere created by the jet engine roar. Heads nodded. Talk ceased. I closed my eyes and dreamed.

Suddenly a voice spoke to me saying, "Why don't you get the new bus? If you use it to uplift me, I will see that you never lose it."

I opened my eyes in surprise and looked discreetly about. Passengers near me were dozing quietly. I was seated alone. No one was near me. But in my heart I knew God had spoken to me, it was the same voice that I had heard in the alcoholic hospital. There could be no mistaking that.

I settled back again, my head resting on the reclined seat. "Praise you, Lord," I said, "praise you, Jesus." A peace descended on me as soft as the fleecy clouds. My mind was totally at ease after such a frustrating day of exploring buses.

An image floated in front of me. There as big as life appeared a bus, exactly like the one I had seen on the lot. I wondered how it would be painted. But then, it turned allowing me to see it was black on top, silver gray elsewhere except for a black band around the middle. Big bold letters emblazoned on the side proclaimed SEGO BROTHERS AND NAOMI.

I smiled to myself. "I think I'll put Sego Brothers and Naomi on the back too, so people can tell who we are coming and going."

The voice pressed gently, "No, don't do that. I'll tell you what to put back there."

For several days I kept the vision to myself trying to decide what to make of it. The chance to tell somebody about it came late one night en route from California. We had just crossed the border into the Texas panhandle from New Mexico traveling Route 66.

Now old enough to drive, Carlton was handling the wheel. I kept him company while the others slept. Cars blinked their lights and whizzed past. "We're going to get a new bus," I said. "The Lord told me that."

"Hmmm," Carlton mumbled as he negotiated the "workhorse" along, never actually commenting on my statement.

The next day, Carlton came back to my compartment where I lay sleeping, and shook me. "Hey, dad," he asked excitedly, "were you kidding me last night? Did you say we're going to get a new bus?"

I sat up in bed and rubbed the sleep from my eyes grinning. "I most definitely did, son."

"But dad, where are you going to get the money?"

"Well, it's like this son. I don't know, but the Lord told me to buy a new bus. So I've got to make an honest effort at it. Since we're in Texas now, why don't we stop in Dallas and see what we can do?"

With mixed feelings, the rest of the group reluctantly went along with my suggestion. Everybody pooled their resources and we scraped together every cent we had on hand. It came to about $2,000—enough for a down payment.

Back in Dallas, I marched right into the place where I had first seen the Silver Eagle and placed an order as if I already had the money in the bank. I knew I could depend on the Lord to supply the balance. After all, He was my heavenly Father, and I felt I had His permission.

I gave the bus company precise instructions for personalizing the Silver Eagle based on my vision. "This is what I want the bus to look like," I announced handing over a rough sketch.

The Segos had just ordered the finest bus that money could buy. Now we had to pay for it. Since it was built in Belgium, it would take a number of months to be ready and shipped. I loaded our schedule with every possible date to have enough money to pay for the bus by the time it arrived.

In the weeks that followed, I pushed myself and the group

into a reckless schedule of dates. Other financial obligations forced me into borrowing a sizeable amount in advances against future royalties from my record company. Since I had perilous trouble with finances in the past, I hated being in debt. The strain nagged and pushed continually at me.

My health was soon affected. One morning I awoke feeling strange and unusually sluggish. I had experienced this sensation frequently during the last several weeks.

I walked into the kitchen where Naomi and W.R. were talking. "I don't feel right," I said weakly. "Something's wrong with me. I believe I'm going to have a stroke."

"James????" Naomi said as she reached out to steady me.

I sat down out of breath and drained of strength. "I think you'd better take me to a hospital," I gasped.

"Are you sure, James?" W.R. asked.

I opened my mouth to explain how I felt, but Naomi and W.R. only stared in amazement, their eyes wide in fright. I couldn't understand their reaction. Although I knew what I was trying to say, I didn't realize that what came out was all garbled and jumbled—like a baby jabbering.

Realizing this was serious, W.R. made a hurried dash outside to his car which contained a citizens band radio and called for an ambulance.

I prayed to God all the way to the hospital, as the ambulance whipped through the winding streets of Nashville, its siren blaring, red lights flashing. The emergency room loomed ahead. I was in a state of shock and confusion by the time I was rolled into a small room.

A doctor flashed a tiny light in my eyes. Nurses moved everywhere. I tried to speak but no one seemed to understand. I became frustrated at my inability to communicate, not knowing this only agitated my condition.

I tried to speak again, but to no avail.

A nurse called out my respiration and pulse rate. "Going down," she said. That's the last thing I remember. I slipped into oblivion for the next seven days.

In the meantime, the Silver Eagle arrived from Belgium. With it came the demand of making a $10,000 payment before taking possession. The situation looked impossible.

Naomi racked her brain for an answer to our financial dilemma. It was now more complicated by my illness which created medical bills into thousands of dollars.

Finally, after much prayer, Naomi decided to prepare a mimeographed letter. Many long hours were spent laboriously addressing envelopes and licking stamps. Each letter found its way to friends on our mailing list explaining our critical situation, my sickness and the need for the new bus.

"The new bus will help us in promoting God's praises in song," Naomi wrote. The letter closed with a request to pray for the Segos and an appeal to consider sending five dollars for a new record, with the proceeds going towards the purchase of the bus.

The response was overwhelming. Friends throughout the country showered their love upon us in a burst of generous giving. About the same time, Lamar decided to buy the "workhorse."

The need was met. God had worked a financial miracle supplying the full amount of $10,000.

Within days of the miracle, I was dismissed from the hospital and allowed to return home. I sat on the front porch waiting as the new Silver Eagle, displaying SEGO BROTHERS AND NAOMI on the side, wheeled onto Cranor Drive and chugged down the street. Although I was unable to travel on the new bus, I was thrilled about it. The doctors insisted I rest for a long period of time before attempting to go back on the road with the group.

Although the down payment had been made on the bus, we

ran into another financial snag. Tennessee law requires payment of a county ad valorem tax on the value of the bus as well as a state sales tax. Once again, we needed several thousand dollars.

This time, friends in gospel singing came to our rescue. Groups like the Oak Ridge Boys, J. D. Sumner and the Stamps, the Statesmen Quartet, the Happy Goodmans and others like Mrs. Lou Hildreath, Wendy Bagwell and J.G. Whitfield, reached deep into their pockets in Christian love and met the balance.

Preachers like the Rev. Jimmie Dobbs of Jacksonville, Florida, helped out. Months earlier he had promised to give $100 towards the bus. When he found out about our need, he promptly sent his check. It seemed as if people came out of the woodwork to help us. In some cases, it was friends we didn't know we had.

"Thank you, Lord," I frequently prayed. "I said I didn't deserve a bus like that. Now I feel I don't deserve friends like these. You used them to bring a miracle to pass."

THIRTEEN
The Visitor Returns

Slowly, weeks passed and my body mended. But just when I had recuperated to the place that I was preparing to once again travel with the group, the plans dissolved in the face of a second stroke. This time more severe than the first.

I felt defeated and alone as I lay once more in an intensive care unit of a Nashville hospital. The blockage of a blood vessel carrying nourishment to my brain caused my usual ruddy complexion to fade to an ashen paleness.

Already despondent over lying in bed for weeks and irritated at my inability to talk, I grew further agitated by the frequent visit of a man from whom I had borrowed monies against royalties. I should have appreciated his concern but I felt he was keeping tabs on me because of the debts.

My financial condition couldn't have looked worse. The hospital bill hovered at the $10,000 mark. God had miraculously supplied the Silver Eagle, but it looked as if He would be pressed to do another miracle as the medical bills soared. I fretted continually over the situation.

Doctors gave my family no hope that I would survive the

second stroke. In case I did live, they offered no chance I'd live any kind of normal life. It looked as if I had become a sudden liability. I wondered if this was the way life would end for me. I wanted to wear out singing the gospel, not pass out in some hospital.

I realized there wasn't much the hospital staff or I could do about my situation. Naomi frequently came to the hospital and prayed over me. Every place the group sang they asked people to pray.

The doctors proceeded with a multitude of tests. The days dragged by. I dreamed of being on the road with the group singing about the Lord. The only melody I had lay unexpressed within the darkness of my mind. Boredom took over.

I turned to television to occupy my thoughts and was soon confronted with the daily problems of soap opera characters. I didn't need more problems but it was a source of entertainment. Besides, I couldn't talk. What else was there to do?

In a few days, I was hooked on the continuing conflicts of "As The World Turns" and "All My Children"—television shows I had once ridiculed were now part of my day.

Several years before, daddy had moved up to Tennessee to live with us. Now he began making regular visits to the hospital. His visits coincided with the soap operas but that didn't bother daddy. He didn't stand for such nonsense. He walked over, firmly clicked off the set, pulled up a chair and opened his well-worn Bible.

"Today," he announced, without asking my permission, "we're going to study about Paul."

In my mute condition, I couldn't object. He looked up to see if I agreed. Submissively, I managed a weak smile. You might say he had a captive audience.

He began to expound the Scriptures making them come

alive. He always marked passages he wanted me to read when I was alone. After an hour or so, he closed the Bible and stood alongside the bed. Then, he placed his rough and leathery hands on my forehead and prayed fervently that God would soon heal me.

Laying the Bible back on the night stand, he'd say, "Now, James, you be sure and read where I showed you." Then, he left.

His visits continued day after day. Our time together became precious but because I was still feeling sorry for myself, it was not until much later that I realized just how much the time meant.

The doctors checked me every day to see if there was any residual damage. "Somehow blood has clogged an artery to your brain leaving only a 10 percent opening through which the blood flows," explained my family doctor. "This has produced the aphasia or loss of the ability to speak which you've experienced."

Feeling that perhaps surgery would best save my life, my doctor called in an arterial specialist and a neurosurgeon. They examined me over several days and agreed that "by-pass surgery" was needed. There was a note of warning. "There is only a fifty-fifty chance of survival with this kind of operation," the doctors suggested.

The surgery was finally scheduled. The night before I lay anxious and uneasy. I knew I was right with God but I worried over the finances. I wanted things better for my family in the event I didn't survive. I knew they'd be burdened by the huge hospital costs plus the debts on the record royalties.

I began to pray. Before long, tears were bathing my face. "Oh, Lord, why did you let this happen to me? This should have happened to somebody else. This shouldn't have happened to me. I ain't wasting money on liquor now, Lord.

All I got is hospital bills."

I wept like a child as I prayed. "Lord, you shouldn't have let this happen to me. I'm doing good now. I'm not drinking. I'm just trying to serve you."

The Lord heard it all. I told him about my failures and my frustrations. I told him about my debts—the thousands of dollars I couldn't pay. I told him about my sickness.

Overwhelmed in my spirit, I sobbed until there were no tears left. I grew quiet. Drained of my emotions, I began to slip into a dream-like trance. The last time I looked at the clock I thought it read 11 P.M. Patients in the rooms near mine had ceased to ring their buzzers. Nurses' trips down the long corridors grew less and less frequent. It was still.

The dreamy state faded from me as I sensed a change take place in the room. I felt a presence. I knew suddenly I wasn't alone any longer. I turned on my side to see who had come in but the door remained shut—as it had been since the nurse's final rounds.

A joy overflooded me. I realized the presence of the Holy Spirit had entered the room. I felt so completely at peace—nothing else mattered. I knew I had touched the throne of God with my prayers. He had heard me.

The brightness grew as though dawn had come and I heard the voice once again—

"I have come back," He said. "I am the one who healed you from drinking. I am the same one who has been with you every day. I am back and I will heal you."

Amidst the Lord's speaking, I floated off into perfect and dreamless sleep. The next morning I felt alert and alive.

Dr. Lanier, one of the specialists, came in to routinely examine me before surgery. I hesitated about speaking, or mentioning my experience the night before.

But I gradually felt urged to talk. As I did, my state of aphasia began regressing. The doctor, fat and jowled, looked surprised as my speech became clearer with each phrase.

"Hmmmmm," he said, "I believe you are saying words you couldn't say before, Mr. Sego."

I felt excitement mounting within me. I sensed the Lord's nearness, but I had no compulsion to explain the previous night's experience to the doctor.

After finishing the examination, he left the room, only to return shortly. "Mr. Sego," he said, "since you have progressed so suddenly in your speech, I believe we will wait and see if there is still further improvement. I don't feel we should operate today. I'll discuss it with the other doctors."

It wasn't long after he left before Dr. Fairchild, one of the other specialists, made his rounds. "Well, Mr. Sego, are you ready for that operation today?" he questioned.

"Oh, what day is it?" I replied.

"It's Wednesday. I'm going to get you ready to be taken to surgery. I'll have the nurse come in and prep you."

I spoke up quickly, "I reckon not—I believe I'll pass on this one."

He glanced at the chart and shook his head. "No, this is the day we scheduled your operation."

"Have you talked to the other doctors?" I asked, looking him straight in the eye.

"No, I haven't."

I grinned. "I think you'd better talk with them, 'cause I think we've got a change in plans."

"Say, you are talking quite well today. Let me have a look at you."

He drew out his instruments from his oversized pockets, laid them on a side table and held a light to my eyes. He proceeded to check me over—from stem to stern.

"You are really talking so much better today," he admitted

when he finished. He paused. "How do you know you aren't going to have this operation?"

"The Lord has healed me," I answered emphatically.

He looked surprised. "Oh, He has, has He?"

He sat down abruptly at the foot of the bed as I moved my legs over to make room. "Are you sure the Lord has done this?"

"Yes, sir," I replied very distinctly. "I'm definitely sure He has. He has touched me and made me whole."

He stood to his feet, patting me on the leg as he rose from the bed. "Well, I'll be going now. See you later."

I watched closely as he turned the corner leaving the room. Tears were in his eyes. My eyes were moist too. I felt the Lord had a reason for telling Dr. Fairchild and not Dr. Lanier. The Great Physician had not only touched me but another physician as well. I prayed neither one of us would ever be the same again.

Naomi was thrilled when she returned from traveling to find me dismissed from the hospital. Her prayers and those of countless others had been answered with my healing.

Somehow the healing had also fired me with a new determination to serve the Lord. I had a persistent urge within me to tell others of the saving, delivering, healing power of the Lord.

With this new zeal, one of the first things I did was get a gospel music show on WSM, the Grand Ole Opry radio station in Nashville. I'd been told there was no way you could get gospel music played on WSM but I felt the Lord could make a way. If we succeeded in getting air time, gospel music as well as the Segos would benefit.

At the station, I met Louie Buck, who was the sales manager. "Hey neighbor, you look familiar," he said smiling. "Don't I know you from somewhere? Where do you come from?"

"You might know me from the Opry or local television," I

answered. "We've been on a lot. But I'm originally from Macon, Georgia."

"Well, well," he said, "I used to be with the Opry. Say did you ever know a guy named Uncle Ned back in Macon?"

"Yeah, sure did," I responded. "I was on his TV program for a number of years."

Buck seemed to warm immediately. "You know, I had him with me back in Atlanta at the Peachtree Hayloft. That was before he went to Macon."

"Is that right?"

"Yeah," he recalled, "Ned was some kind of man. Too bad he's gone. There just aren't enough like him around any more."

My friendship with Uncle Ned appeared to be a bridge. "I've been told there ain't no way you can get on WSM with gospel music. Is that right?"

"You probably heard right," he agreed, "but I tell you what, let's go in and talk with the station management. Maybe we can work something out."

I had barely arrived home from seeing the folks at WSM than Buck was on the phone. "The station has given approval to your gospel music program," he said. "Congratulations!"

Within days, gospel music was being broadcast across the far-reaching voice of WSM. Somehow the Lord had used my association with Uncle Ned to open a door that had been closed to others—but once opened, the gospel benefited.

FOURTEEN

Daddy Walt Goes Home

Gradually, I resumed my road travels with the group. Only this time I tried to pace myself—getting enough rest, the right food and such. I also vowed to spend more time relaxing when I wasn't traveling. At first, I couldn't even sing because of the after effects of the stroke, so the sound man gave me a "dead" microphone. I went on stage with the group and sang into the lifeless mike until I got my raspy voice back. In time, it returned.

During one such period of being off the road, in 1974, daddy suffered a paralyzing stroke. For several years, he had been bothered by heart trouble and mild seizures. But this was serious.

Here was a chance, I decided, to repay him for the many hours he had spent with me. At eighty-two, daddy's hair was completely white, his face lined and wrinkled. In spite of his years, daddy was much the same man I'd always known. Warm. Friendly. Loving.

He had a quality about himself, a sameness that was Christlike. No matter how the fortunes of life turned—either good or bad—daddy was the same. He had found a secret in following Jesus that cushioned his life enabling him to handle whatever came along.

Mama was fond of telling a story about daddy. Long before I was born, when daddy was working at a sawmill, he stopped in the middle of the day to go pray about a matter. The sawmill operator being a man of the world didn't understand this and he slapped my daddy over leaving his work to go pray.

Now daddy's three brothers were a rough-and-tumble bunch. Being of Irish-German extraction, they had fierce tempers. Also working at the sawmill, they saw what happened. In short order, they had the mill owner on the back of a horse and ready to be strung up.

"Wait a minute, boys," daddy shouted. "Hold your peace. God will fight my battles. He'll take care of everything needing to be cared for. I've got somebody bigger than you guys fighting for me."

His brothers reluctantly released the man. The experience made a lasting impression on him. Sometime later, the sawmill owner's fifteen-year-old son got tangled up in a buzz saw and was killed instantly. The sawmill owner, a bullish figure of a man, was greatly disturbed over his son's death.

"I wouldn't worry about it no more," daddy told him one day, "the boy's gone to heaven."

"How'd you know?" the man asked in a broken voice.

"Why I talked to him," daddy responded gently. "He accepted Jesus as his Savior. The same thing you ought to do."

The woods were quiet as daddy and the sawmill operator knelt in the sawdust to pray. None of it probably would have ever happened if daddy hadn't had the character of Christ in him.

I sat and talked with him for hours. One day it occurred to me that daddy was probably the only man who'd never let me down. It seemed like I had been disappointed countless times by others. Many probably felt the same about me. But daddy was different.

Once when mama and daddy were traveling evangelists in the early 1930s, he had to work a part-time job to help feed the family. I was to meet him at the town grocery store to help get groceries home. I was shocked when I saw him purchasing a plug of Ripple chewing tobacco at the counter. He turned around after paying the clerk, and saw me staring—my mouth agape.

"What's the matter, Brother?" he asked kiddingly. "Don't you like tobacco?"

I was crushed and began crying.

Then he grabbed me close. "Don't worry, Brother," he assured me. "I promised to pick this up for some guy I work with. This plug don't belong to me."

You cannot imagine the relief I felt. I shouted and skipped all around him as we walked back up the dusty road together.

Daddy's love and compassion didn't stop at his own family though. Sometimes he went down to Macon to visit relatives and preach in the church he and mama had built. Word spread among the neighborhood's kids about his visit. When daddy arrived in Macon, kids of all ages were lined up at the bus depot to meet "Daddy Walt."

He was prepared, too. He stepped off the bus and began magically pulling packs of gum out of various pockets, teasing the boys and girls all the time. Sometimes as many as fifteen or twenty kids would show up at the bus station to greet him.

During the dark times of the early 1960s when I stayed drunk constantly, daddy never gave up. He stood behind me in prayer. Somehow he believed God was going to deliver me. Many times I awoke from a drunken stupor to find him kneeling beside the bed with his hands on me begging God "to deliver my boy."

It embarrassed and even iritated me when I found daddy praying over me like that. But that was just his way. He never criticized or condemned me for my drinking. His love and concern was always the same, but his prayers bore deep within me.

Back in 1967, I had insisted he move in with us because of his advancing age. His presence over the next seven years proved to be a blessing that's still with me. Daddy had been preaching since two years after he and mama married in 1914. I thought it was time he ought to retire from preaching. He quickly let me know different.

"There ain't no place in the world for a retired preacher, son," he said, fingering the pages of his worn Bible. "It makes me sick to see some preachers retire. If God calls you to preach, He doesn't just one day uncall you."

"I don't quite understand."

"Well, I know the difference between retiring from pastoring a church and retiring from preaching," he explained. "I'm sad to say many preachers look at the ministry as a profession. And like other occupations, when they reach sixty or sixty-five, they want to retire and move to Florida—maybe live the life of Riley."

"Oh," I answered.

"As long as I've got a voice to speak and limbs to carry me, I'm gonna tell people about Jesus," he announced. "But every God-called preacher is called for life—not to just age sixty-five."

Daddy was serious about that. Although his pulpit ministry was over, he still delivered the gospel message wherever possible. When he couldn't get out of the house, he'd take out the telephone book and start down the page making calls.

If somebody answered on the other end, daddy identified himself as a preacher. "I won't bother you long," he'd say, "but

I want to tell you Jesus is coming soon. You need to know that. I wonder if you're ready for His coming?"

Many times people hung up hastily. Others responded and accepted Jesus as their Savior. They were touched that someone would call to tell them about the Lord's coming. For weeks, daddy invited people over to the house just to hear the gospel story.

While on the road singing, there were countless times that I would call home without success—the line was always busy. I thought it was out of order, until I got home. "Daddy, is there anything wrong with the phone?" I questioned.

"No," he answered with a smile. "I've just been calling people."

After that, I got daddy his own telephone line. He needed it for his calling ministry and I needed a way to call home uninterrupted. We were both happy with the results of the two lines.

But he suffered that last debilitating stroke and became bedridden. I decided to begin reading the Bible to him. "Now today, let's talk about Paul," I said. He smiled.

But instead of improving, his condition worsened. I admitted him to a hospital. I tried calling him daily even when I was traveling. Weeks passed. One day he called me. His voice was so weak I could hardly hear him. "Son," he said, "I'm going home."

"Pop, that's great. I'll be right over to get you."

"No, son. I'm going home."

"Pop, I don't understand. What are you talking about? You mean you aren't coming back to my house?"

"That's right, son. I'm really going home. I'm going to be with my Jesus."

That was the last conversation I ever had with him. The next day, James Walter Sego, preacher of the gospel, went home to be with Jesus.

The church was simple, white and small. We followed the coffin down in front of the pulpit. As everyone took their seats, I glanced around the auditorium. It was filled with people, many I didn't know.

The preacher talked glowingly about daddy, but nothing he said equaled the presence of these people. Many had traveled several hundred miles to honor Walt Sego, a preacher who loved them as his own family. Several people paused outside to tell me they had been converted to Christ through daddy's phone ministry.

How I thanked God that daddy never retired.

I followed the slow-winding procession out to the little cemetery, waiting for the pallbearers to precede me to daddy's final resting place. The country church's bell pealed.

The preacher spoke words of comfort and life. "We shall not all sleep. We shall be changed at the last trump. . . ."

My eyes were dry as they lowered the casket into the red clay grave. I was calm and confident. "He's made it," I thought of daddy. "He's gotten his crown. What he suffered is not to be compared with the glory he now has. He's getting to see his King."

Over his life, daddy had suffered through many trials and circumstances. But his work bore much fruit. From the folks saved and the countless lives changed under his ministry, to the Sego Brothers and Naomi's work, daddy's presence bore good fruit. I guess daddy was in my mind when the Segos put together this song.

We shall reach that City bright where the Saviour is the light,
Praise His name forever, we shall wear a shining crown;
We shall walk the streets of gold and a mansion there behold,
When we lay our burdens down.

With the angel choir above we shall sing redeeming love,
We'll receive a shining crown;
There our loved ones we shall meet, and our joys will be
complete,
On that morning when we lay our heavy burdens down.

Heaven's bells will sweetly chime,
Over yonder in that bright and happy, sunny clime;
Ever we shall wear a shining crown,
When we lay our burdens down.

FIFTEEN

Jesus Alone Satisfies

Over the years, I saw many rising stars come and go in gospel music. Some moved on to success and fame. Others trailed off down a lonely road into obscurity. Some were outright sinners. Some were real saints.

In Nashville, I met the largest variety of them all. Kids from all over the nation trudge there every year with a guitar and some songs hoping to make it big. The town is filled with recording studios, talent agencies, success stories—and busted dreams.

The business is dog-eat-dog in many ways. Careers rise and fall with the success of that latest record. Fast buck artists abound, so do people with drinking and drug problems.

Many gospel singers chose unwittingly to imitate people who have attained stardom in secular music. I guess I have strong feelings about that. I've learned its not the glitter of the costume or the antics on stage that produce results. It's the anointing of God that makes the difference.

There's one story that best exemplifies what I'm saying. It seems as if it were only yesterday when it unfolded.

"Brother James, I have a little boy who likes to sing," I heard a man's voice telling me over the phone. It was 1958, a time in the music world when country and western was declining in popularity and gospel was flourishing.

"Well, brother, that's good, but I really don't have an outlet to help him at this time," I tried to explain. "What do you think I could do to help him?"

"Well, I understand your group will be appearing at a singing tonight at a Baptist church out on Napier Avenue," he replied. "Can we come over and maybe you could let him sing a song?"

"Sure," I answered, "I'll be glad to do that."

The church was filled to capacity when we arrived. A man walked up holding the hand of a blond-headed kid who looked to be five or six. He identified himself as Frank Edwards, the man who had called me earlier, and his son, Eddie. I thought the kid looked like anything but a singer. "Go ahead and find a seat," I suggested, "and we'll call on you later."

The crowd was enthusiastic and lively. We sang about forty-five minutes and needed to catch a breath. I thought it would be a good time to see what the kid could do, and called him up. "What are you going to sing, young man?" I asked.

He politely told me the name of the song, but added, "I'll have to have my father play for me because he knows the song the way I sing it."

The small boy was confident. I looked at him and smiled. Dressed in a blue suit and bow tie, I noticed his slicked down hair, clear trusting eyes and sweet manner. "This is either gonna be a disaster or something big," I thought to myself.

"Okay, son, go ahead," I motioned him toward the microphone.

He walked over unabashedly as his father sat down at the piano and began to play. I was all ears. But as the kid sang, I was shocked. A beautiful and clear tenor voice came from the small youngster. I'd never heard such sweet music before from so young a child.

"Wow," I thought, "if I was ever in a place needing a kid singer, this boy would be it."

Eddie finished his song. Before I could step up and thank him, he'd already announced another one. I was tickled. He was only supposed to sing one. Instead, he sang three or four. But his voice was so appealing, I didn't mind. Neither did anybody else.

The group began to hum softly behind him. When he finished, I stepped up. "Do that first one over again and we'll sing along with you."

Hearing the group behind him gave the boy more confidence and he belted the song out. The audience was enthralled. When he finished, the people arose all over the auditorium in a standing ovation.

Eddie's father agreed for us to take the kid with us on our next series of engagements. I felt his talents were outstanding and realized he needed someone to open a few doors for him. After all, there were pitfalls I hoped to shield the kid from.

When our next recording session was scheduled in Nashville, we took him along again. The Lord anointed us extra and we finished our session early that day. I realized I still had time left on the six hour sessions I had already bought. "Maybe the Lord wants this kid to record a few songs," I pondered.

I walked over to the session engineer. "Say, man, I've got this kid with me I told you about earlier," I reminded him. "You told me I could record him if he's recordable. The group knows the vocal backup on his songs and I'd like to see him cut a single record today on the extra time we have left." The engineer agreed.

I called Eddie over and explained what we were going to do.

The group formed, the machines were set, then the engineer gave Eddie his cue. I was amazed. He sang completely at ease. I'd never seen anybody handle their first recording session quite like that. Most folks get what I call "the nervous tizzies." Not Eddie, he was calm and collected.

The record was cut on the first take.

Several weeks later, Eddie accompanied us on our first appearance in Atlanta. People accepted the Sego Brothers and Naomi that night with open arms. There was something dynamic about the crowd's response to our singing.

After several numbers, I asked, "How'd you folks like to hear the best little boy singer I've ever heard?"

I think I could have sold the crowd on anything that night. They clapped and shouted, "Bring him on."

The crowd must have been surprised when such a small boy walked out on stage. A hush fell. Eddie must have looked lost on the platform to some folks in the audience.

I'd never heard such a large auditorium get so quiet as when Eddie clutched the microphone and began singing, "Down on My Knees." At six, this kid was a professional. He knelt down on the apron of the stage and poured his heart out in song.

The old city auditorium with its two tiers of balconies was filled with almost seven thousand people. I knew there couldn't have been a dry eye in the place. As he finished, the auditorium echoed with the sounds of cheers and applause. My eyes were even moist. But Eddie stood there listening to the jubilant cheers without showing any emotion.

We had only five hundred copies of Eddie's record with us. They sold out immediately. We probably could have sold a thousand more, it seemed.

After the auditorium emptied and the equipment was loaded, everybody filed on the bus talking excitedly about Eddie's success. "How do you feel?" I asked him as the bus rolled out of the city.

"Good," he said smiling. "I felt just like somebody was holding me up when I stood up there in front of those people. I don't know how to say it but that's what I felt."

I returned the smile. "Did you feel like the Lord was with you?" I questioned.

"Oh, yes," he said, turning his big shining eyes on me.

We rolled down Highway 41 back towards Macon. The bus grew quiet except for the sounds of the road. W.R. dozed in his seat. "You know what?" Eddie said thoughtfully.

"What?"

"I never dreamed this could happen to me."

Eddie's manner was always warm and charming. Never once did he display ill manners or a brattish temper. As our own demand increased because of our records, Eddie traveled along with us for as often as ten days in a row.

As audiences continually responded to Eddie's singing, I recognized the Lord had touched this boy in a special way. Naomi seemed to understand these things better than me. I asked her one day about him. "There's something about that boy," I said. "When he sings something moves and motivates inside of me."

"Well," she responded, "I think it's because he is a special anointed vessel of God. Even though he's so young, the Lord has placed something special on him."

"Yeah, that must be it."

"It's always there when he sings," Naomi suggested, "and you can see the people feel it too. They wouldn't respond so warmly otherwise."

Eddie soon found he could trust me and we talked often and freely about everything. I knew I wasn't a father replacement, just a special friend. Eddie knew I cared.

My kids grew to love him too. They enjoyed times together

and treated him like a member of the family. He spent many hours playing at the house or sharing a meal at our table. But Eddie also felt a kind of loneliness. He was a kid who had been thrust into an adult world of auditoriums, gospel sings, record sessions and travel. But he was still a kid. He sorely missed things like football, baseball and hunting. He accepted the fact he was different, yet he felt deprived in many ways.

One night backstage in Johnson City, Tennessee, I looked out from behind the curtains into an auditorium packed with almost 15,000 people. I had been told a Broadway producer was in the crowd to consider Eddie for a role in a play.

I drew him to me and pointed out through the closed curtains. "Eddie, out there somewhere is a guy from New York who wants to hear you. I want you to do your best tonight."

I needn't have worried about Eddie. He was now ten years old, but he was as professional as anybody on the stage. In some ways, he was better.

After the program ended, the Broadway producer talked with Eddie and his father. In a matter of days, Eddie left for Connecticut where he began work in a play. Although the production never made Broadway, producers discovered the boy's special talent and he graduated into an acting career. He appeared in a western movie and did several programs on television.

Almost two years passed before I heard anything from Eddie. By that time, he had traveled full circle and was back in gospel singing. He was signed for a popular gospel music show and began recording for one of the top gospel record labels.

For a year or so, his popularity was at its zenith. But by the time he reached thirteen an event took place that is totally unique and frustrating to boys. His voice changed.

Further complications developed for Eddie when his backup group sensed his career was over and left. At fourteen, most insiders considered his career washed-out. When he attempted to sing, his voice squeaked and cracked. It varied from high to low.

One night I spotted Eddie sadly watching groups perform from the wings of a stage in Dothan, Alabama. I was glad to see him, walked over and placed my arm around him. "How are you, boy?"

"I guess I'm all right, Brother Sego," he said dismally. "But I can't sing anymore."

"Young man," I said patiently, "when the Lord gives you a voice, He doesn't take it away. Just be still and wait. He's coming back with something else for you."

He smiled weakly, encouraged at my words.

About six months later, Eddie's voice took on a beautiful but lower quality. It still had a magnetic touch though. Once again, he sold records by the score. Practically every album he made produced several single records. I worked at singings where many times he sold twice as many records as we did.

His popularity jetted him into a different plane of the gospel music world—an upper echelon where few groups or individual singers reach.

I saw Eddie from time to time when our paths crossed. On those occasions, I'd slap him on the back and give him a bear hug. "How are you doin', boy?" I always asked, letting him know my concern. "I still love you."

He always replied, "I love you too."

But I noticed something troubling him. "What's up?"

"Well, I don't know," he said looking for words to explain his feelings. "I just seem to sense a lot of jealousy when I'm around some of the groups. I guess some of the people are threatened by the way my records sell. Folks either ignore me or badmouth me. I don't really understand it."

I tried to talk to Eddie, explaining that those kinds of people are in every stratum of life, including gospel music. "They're kinda like the poor. Jesus said we'd always have them with us. I think we'll always have the others too. You can't let it get you down though. All of us just have to learn how to cope with it."

Eddie knew I was right, but he still didn't know how to handle the frustrations involved. He began to change. Forces seemed to be at work in his life almost the way alcohol attacked mine. Something seemed to poison his mind. Many times I wished he was still within the protective environs of our bus.

Professional jealousy soon overwhelmed him. Finding it too hard to compete any more, he turned to his father one day. "I'm through," he said with a note of finality. "I'm tired of making a living this way. I've done it all my life. I've never done my own thing. I've never done what I want to do, but now I am."

And with that, he walked out.

His father called me, extremely upset. I had no words of real comfort. I had seen it coming years before. "I promise, we'll pray," was all I could say.

Time passed. I thought I'd never hear from Eddie again. I was surprised when I answered the doorbell at home one day to find him standing outside. I couldn't believe the change in him when he announced, "It's me, Eddie. Don't you recognize me?"

"Yeah, Eddie," I answered trying not to show outright shock. "It's good to see you. Come on in."

I couldn't help staring at his long, unkempt hair and dirty patched jeans. Somehow I found myself looking for traces of that little blond-headed boy I'd known years ago. It was obvious that Eddie was living in a world far removed from his roots.

He took a seat opposite me. I looked sadly into his eyes that were once filled with the innocence of youth. They were now glassy and dull, obviously from drugs. He appeared high from something. "What's he looking for?" I asked myself.

"We sure miss hearing you sing songs about the Lord," I remarked.

"You know," he said matter-of-factly, "I found out there was more to life than those songs I used to sing. There's a lot more than just serving one god. There are a lot more religions and other ways to serve God. Jesus is just one of the gods the world has to offer. There's good in them all."

I shook my head. "Listen to me, Eddie," I said. "These other guys—Buddha, Mohammed, Krishna—they're all dead. They didn't die for your sins either. Jesus did. And Jesus, the one you used to sing about—He still lives today."

He dropped his head, trying to avoid my eyes. The room was silent for a moment. When he looked back again, I thought I saw his eyes shining—ever so briefly.

"Yeah, I know that," he said softly. "But some of these people who are singing gospel, they say they're serving God. But if that's serving the Lord, I decided I didn't want any part of it."

"I agree, Eddie," I said sympathetically. "I've been through those disappointments myself. People will disappoint you, but Jesus won't. Somehow you just can't put your confidence in folks. They're human. They stumble and fall. You have to put your faith and confidence in Jesus. He's the only one who can't fail."

"That don't change people though, does it?"

"No, it won't," I answered, "but it'll change you. That way you can learn to function and handle such problems."

Eddie was quiet. "Jesus is alive," I said gently. "He can live in your heart. You can come alive too, Eddie, if you'll just turn your life back over to Him."

The statement hung in mid air. He neither bought or

rejected it. I finally convinced Eddie to spend several days and visit with Carlton. But he was soon restless and ready to leave.

"Thanks, Brother Sego. Be seeing you around."

"I hate to see you leave. What are you going to be doing?" I asked.

"Oh, I'm with a group that just did a new rock-n-roll record," he exclaimed. "It's great. We just spent thirty hours in a studio perfecting it."

"Well, you know the right road, Eddie," I said. "One day I know you'll take it." He didn't comment. "I hope you'll write to me," I suggested.

He reached in his wallet and pulled out a printed card. "Here. This is my phone number. If you ever need to get in touch with me, call me. I don't always talk on the phone, though, unless I know who's calling. I get a lot of calls from promoters and record companies trying to get me back in gospel."

I looked at the card. Eddie was advertised as a studio musician in Atlanta. He left my home that day still not walking with God. Days later I received a copy of his record. To my dismay, it was just country songs pitched to a rock-n-roll beat. Eddie was now doing his own thing, but I knew it would never satisfy.

There were others like Eddie. Some were young, looking for a break in the business. They came, rode my bus to get the feel of the road, and then moved on. Others came trying to get the busted pieces of their lives mended. Many knew I'd been a drunk and sought help from me. Johnny Jay was one such case.

Johnny had been a fine bass singer with a midwestern quartet for over fifteen years. He was just a casual drinker at first, but in time, like me, Johnny became an alcoholic. Finally, the group fired him. His marriage hung in the balance.

For several months, Johnny traveled with us. In time, he

was able to surrender his life to Christ and quit drinking. His marriage was saved. Soon afterwards, Johnny left the road for a nine-to-five job. He's happy now. So is his family.

Everybody in gospel music isn't like Eddie or Johnny. Most of the professional Christian entertainers with whom I'm acquainted are honest, conscientious, hard-working people. But, as with anything of value, there is always a counterfeit. The enemy of our soul will be sure of that.

Many who have known my story have asked how could somebody sing gospel music and be an alcoholic. That same question could be posed to Johnny or many others. Or why does somebody like Eddie choose to leave gospel music?

The answer is actually tied into the nature of gospel music. When an auditorium is full, a singer's spirits soar as he steps into the lights and listens to the thundering applause of thousands. Throughout the performance, the singer has a feeling of exhilaration.

But once the last fan has gone home, a note of depression often sets in as the singer realizes it's over for the night. An empty auditorium can be one of the loneliest places in the world for a singer. There's nothing left to do but load up the equipment and move on to the next town. Traveling brings on another set of problems. Many times, it's a physical grind.

In the process, few people can take the stress and strain of performing and traveling. It's an emotional drain. To fill that void, many pop pills or drink. Others lose themselves with women. Only a few can survive. And some of the few who survive, like Eddie, are spoiled by what they see.

For me, I've found Jesus is the only one who can fill the void in my life. He alone satisfies. He alone can help.

SIXTEEN
Born to Sing

"You'll always be a success as long as you remember your talents are God-given," mama reminded me many years ago. "Without Him, you're absolutely nothing."

Her words have had a prophetic ring to them over the years as Naomi, W.R. and myself have learned that whatever success we've achieved, as well as our singing voices, are all God-given. Our fifty-three record albums have sold in excess of two million copies. Last year alone, our traveling took us over 100,000 miles to virtually every state in the Union except Alaska and Hawaii. The Sego's gave 365 performances during 1976—sometimes as often as three or four a day.

Over the years, we've gone to small churches in the backwoods and larger churches on Main Street. I never refused to go because of the size of the church or amount of the offering. All that was needed was a place where a group of people wanted to hear the gospel sung.

That kind of approach in going places to sing has produced provocative situations with people, mostly preachers or promoters. I've had preachers meet me at their church doors to check out my doctrine. If his church doesn't believe in the rapture, he might tell me not to sing any songs about it. Or he might quiz me about drinking, smoking, or my position on divorce.

And then, there can be problems about money. Once we were in a packed church in North Carolina. The crowd looked to be close to a thousand people. After we sang for about thirty minutes, the preacher, a tall and lanky man, stood to announce the offering.

"These people are worthy of everything we can give 'em," he told the enthusiastic crowd. "They give themselves hundreds of days a year to sing the gospel. We really want to bless 'em for coming here."

His inspiring pitch lasted for some twenty minutes. I didn't think much of it until the ushers began moving among the crowd for the offering. Only, they weren't using regular offering plates. They had red and white Kentucky Fried Chicken buckets.

Something snapped in the back of my mind. Another gospel singer had told me recently about coming from a church in North Carolina where the offering had been taken in KFC buckets. "But the preacher skimmed it considerably before I got it," he told me. "If you ever go there, watch yourself."

"This must be the place," it suddenly occurred to me.

The ushers were coming down the aisles now. The buckets were full. I had to do something. Hurriedly, I got on my feet. "You gonna give that to us, ain't you?" I said to the preacher who was looking at the ushers coming forward.

"Yeah," he answered.

"Fine," I said, turning to the ushers who were now beside me. "Tell you what, let's just stack it here on the altar and we'll go on singing. We thank you for your generosity."

"But, uh . . ." the preacher stuttered, looking confused.

I motioned the group to take their places. "Let's sing," I said commandingly. We finished the program. I picked up the buckets from the altar and headed for the bus.

Within minutes, the preacher who now appeared angry, was knocking on the bus door. "You gonna give me my buckets back?" he asked.

"Sure," I said, handing him the empty buckets.

"You gonna tell me how much the offering was?"

"Sure," I answered, writing down the amount on a slip of paper and handing it to him.

He looked at the figures. "You know we ain't gonna need you here any more," he volunteered.

"Yes sir, I figured as much."

"Just remember that," he said, stomping off the bus.

Even though there are plenty of preachers and promoters like that man who want to take advantage—there are many others who will bend over backwards to be honest and fair. I don't sing because of either group. I sing because God has put it in my heart.

At times, a man who has suffered two strokes and years of alcoholism gets weary. One night in Asheville, North Carolina, I walked to the rear of the auditorium and slumped down in a cushioned seat, tired and weary. We had sung our best that night.

The custodian was turning off the lights. His crew was closing the place down. Strewn about the auditorium were the leftovers of the concert. Crumpled programs. Soft drink cups with rivulets of water from melted ice. Popcorn dotting the seat and lying flattened on the carpet.

I realized many lives had converged on the auditorium for a few hours' time. Now they were all gone. Some returning to homes filled with sadness. Others to happy ones. What had we been able to do for these people? Anything of real value?

I rose to leave the auditorium. The lobby was now deserted except for litter scattered about. A brief time before, the place had been congested with people at the record displays purchasing albums from various groups.

Everybody was on the bus. I settled back listening to the husky droning of the Silver Eagle's diesel. "Was it all worth it?" I wondered. "The travel, the hassle, the sacrifice of being away from home all these days and nights."

I thought of the audience's response. I thought of the people who'd been drawn closer to Jesus. I remembered the ninety-six people who'd been saved in a single week's time when we sang in an Ohio revival service.

"Yes, it's worth it," I decided. "In spite of all the frustrations, the misunderstandings, the problems, it's worth it. There's an eternal value to it all." The Silver Eagle roared off into the night toward our next concert.

Thirty-eight years have passed since that twelve-year-old boy sat listening to the Smile-A-While Quartet. His prayer of "Lord, let me sing just like them" has long since been answered.

The Lord kindled a flame in that boy's heart that would never go out. The flame was a burning desire to sing the gospel. Many times the flame flickered. At times, it was almost extinguished by temptations, discouragement, heartaches, even near death. But God stayed close. No matter how great the storm, the fire burned on.

If you're ever in one of our concerts, you'll see me standing behind a microphone blending my raspy tenor voice with Naomi's trumpet-like alto and W.R.'s mellow baritone. Most likely, I'll be smiling as I sing along. You may find yourself wondering, "Is that smile real, or is that part of Sego's stage routine?"

Let me assure you, though my teeth are false, my smile is genuine. Man, I'm doing what I always wanted to do. I was born to sing the gospel.

APPENDIX

Alcoholism and drunkenness are not the same. Many persons may get drunk, but are not alcoholics. Some people drink to be sociable. Alcoholics drink because they must. The urge to drink is so strong he can't control it. James Sego was an alcoholic.

Doctors who have studied alcoholism for years still don't know the real reasons why alcoholics drink. Studies indicate many drink to escape from tensions, frustrations and anxieties. The true alcoholic believes only alcohol can make life bearable.

There are a number of ways to treat the alcoholic. A few include such diverse treatments as with drugs, psychotherapy and groups like Alcoholics Anonymous (A.A.).

I have no vast storehouse of knowledge on alcoholics or alcoholism. But having spent many years drinking and being hospitalized, I do have some practical suggestions to offer. If you know someone who is an alcoholic or if you're one yourself, these suggestions may be of help to you.

First of all, you need to present this person's case to the Lord like my wife did mine. You must pray diligently. That prayer might not be answered in a week, a month or maybe even a year. It may take many years. But it will be answered.

Secondly, always let the alcoholic know he is loved. These people need more love than the average person because of the private hell they live in. You should never give an alcoholic the impression he isn't loved or cared for.

Thirdly, let this person know that Jesus Christ loves him, that Jesus Christ understands his problem, and that Jesus Christ cares for him. Always point the person toward the Lord as the ultimate answer to all of man's needs.

Fourthly, if professional care is needed for the person, get help for him but do it with love and concern. Don't slap him in a hospital as a hurtful way of paying the alcoholic back for the trouble he may have caused you.

Fifthly, if you find any whiskey around the house, don't pour it out. Most non-drinkers would automatically do that. As a former alcoholic, that would have made me resentful and I'd have soon found transportation and money to buy some more. Most drinkers feel this way, so save yourself some money.

And last, remember a person is not himself when under the influence of alcohol. He doesn't even realize the situation he's in. Bear that in mind as you deal with an alcoholic.

These suggestions might sound simplistic and even illogical. But believe me, they work. I'm living proof of that.